9-30-01
For Karen —
Best Wishes
Ruth Long

GOOD PEOPLE
The Whole Self Integration Guide

GOOD PEOPLE

The Whole Self Integration Guide

RUTH CHERRY, Ph.D.

Copyright © 1990 by Ruth Cherry

Cover photo copyright by Melvin L. Harris
Cover and book design by Melvin L. Harris and Susan Muller-Harris
Cover artwork by Phil Morel
Type composition by Melvin L. Harris and Susan Muller-Harris
Copyediting by Laura Norvig

All rights reserved. No part of this work may be reproduced or transmitted in any form by any means, electronic or mechanical, including photocopying and recording, or by any information storage and retrieval system without written permission from the publisher:

IBS PRESS
744 Pier Avenue
Santa Monica, CA 90405
(213)450-6485

IBS PRESS FIRST PRINTING, JUNE, 1990

Library of Congress Cataloging-in-Publication Data
Cherry, Ruth.
    Good People : the whole-self integration guide / by Ruth Cherry.
      p. cm.
    ISBN 0-9616605-7-0 : $10.95
    1. Self-talk—Case studies. 2. Subconsciousness—Case studies.
3. Self-realization—Case studies. 4. Self-talk—Problems,
exercises, etc. 5. Subconsciousness—Problems, exercises, etc.
6. Self-realization—Problems, exercises, etc. I. Title.
BF697.5.S47C44   1990
158'.1—dc20   90-36709
                                                                  CIP

ISBN 0-9616605-7-0

Manufactured in the United States of America

special thanks to
Mary Ricker

Publisher's Note

This publication is designed to provide accurate and authoritative information in regard to the subject matter covered. It is sold with the understanding that the publisher is not engaged in rendering psychological, medical, or other professional services. If expert assistance or counseling is needed, the services of a competent professional should be sought.

Editor's Note

The case studies in this book, while drawn from Dr. Cherry's extensive therapeutic experience, are composites with fictional names.

Because the English language lacks a genderless pronoun to use in place of "he or she," and because the majority of Dr. Cherry's clients happen to be women, feminine pronouns are sometimes used in this text in a general sense and are meant to refer to humans of both genders.

Contents

Foreword		*vii*
Introduction		*xi*
How to Use This Book		*xx*
1	Good People	1
2	The Control/Compliance Game	11
3	Our Lives are Projections	45
4	Developing a Caring Parent	81
5	Relationships are Reflections	105
6	Listening to the Body	127
7	Healing Addiction	151
8	Listening to Spirit	175
Afterword		193
Glossary		197

Foreword

For years therapists have been writing books for other therapists on the paradigm of subpersonalities, while most of the general public has been completely unaware of the dynamics and structure of this internal system. For that reason, *Good People* is long overdue. It is written in a clear style, free of professional jargon, and will help you understand your inner life.

Sigmund Freud developed the dynamic concept of the mind, defining the functions and interactions of our personal conscious and unconscious systems. Then Carl Jung described the collective unconscious. Roberto Assagioli, the founder of psychosynthesis, personalized the concept, teaching clients to access and actualize individual parts of themselves in order to reach the inner core—the consciousness of Self.

Synthesis is the combining of parts to form a whole, and the psychosynthesis of subpersonalities comes in several stages. The first is recognition of the primary subpersonalities in play during personal conflict in an individual's life. The second step is acceptance of these parts. The premise of psychosynthesis is that all parts of us are intrinsically good. As we begin to gestalt the parts of who we are, we often find that the repressed or "shadow" parts that seem to act out in a destructive way, once accessed and understood, become the creative or spontaneous parts of who we are. Conversely, the parts we thought were "good" often seem judgmental, punitive and harmful to the system as a whole, when seen in this new light.

The next stage is coordination, and to negotiate this we have to access our inherently positive parts: the Healthy Adult, the Wise Person, the Earth Mother, the Objective Observer; the balanced core of who we are. We then integrate the parts of ourselves with time-sharing, cooperation, understanding, communication, so all parts of us feel safe and have opportunities for self-expression. The ultimate level of the process is synthesis—refinement and harmonization of the Self.

Good People provides processes to access and work with our primary subpersonalities. Dr. Cherry clearly demonstrates with questions and case histories how to create lines of communication to the repressed parts, and between the disparate parts. She models in this book the different stages of psychosynthesis of the Self, and deftly integrates Transactional Analysis, gestalt, "inner child" and subpersonality work.

She shows us how to identify the Wounded Child—the needy, demanding or abandoned Child that so many of us carry suppressed within us. This Child is usually punitively repressed by the Judge, Critic, Controller or the "Good Person." How can we heal the Child if we don't know or understand the parts of us who shame the Child? How do we heal the Child if we can't access the healthy, gentle, or caring Parent? If we exhibit compulsive-addictive behavior, we need to understand that only parts of us are compulsive, not the entire system. To identify the parts that need to eat or drink or obsess and get them working with the healthy parts is the road to recovery. We can stop abuse if we understand the dynamics of the co-dependent abuse triangle, in which the roles of victim, rescuer and perpetrator are constantly interchanged.

In *Good People*, Dr. Cherry shows us that to neglect any part of ourselves is to limit our emotional growth and the expansion of our own awareness. She gives us the understanding and the tools to awaken our buried monsters, struggle through conflicts, and discover true strength. This book is about the journey within, where we listen to our own truths, trust what we hear and find a peaceful balance.

TRICIA CAETANO, B.A.
Founder, Personal Development Center
San Diego, CA

Introduction

In my work with clients over the past fourteen years, I have noticed recurrent themes. People want to live meaningful, satisfying lives but are confused about how to do so. They rely on early teachings and their observations of authority figures, but eventually feel frustration and disappointment with this approach. Their experience conflicts with their expectations, and the resulting pain and anger further clouds their views of the world and of themselves.

For most of us, what we were taught to do or to be as children doesn't work to make us safe and happy as adults. Being "nice" doesn't guarantee us a peaceful marriage. Being "fair" doesn't insure that others will deal with us responsibly. When we have done all the "good" things we are "supposed" to do and truly act the role of a "good person" and we are still unhappy, frustrated or disappointed, we begin to question our beliefs. "If I'm doing everything right," we wonder, "why is life so difficult?"

The results of this confusion and frustration are evident in such common physical disorders as anorexia, bulimia, chronic overeating, alcoholism, drug abuse, compulsive exercise, psychosomatic complaints, sleep disorders, chronic muscle tension, headaches and sexual dysfunction. Depression, worry, excessive busyness and fatigue are indications of psychological imbalance. The symptoms of imbalance are widespread and grossly apparent, but the underlying unconscious conflicts which cause them are poorly understood.

The unconscious is an important part of each of us, but one with which few of us are acquainted. We have not learned to respect or to value those processes in us which are hidden and are not "rational." Our culture values the apparent and the tangible, but denies the individual's psychological and spiritual needs. Yet, there is more to us than our conscious minds. A large part of each of us is not intellectual or focused or self-willed. What we would like to be and to present to the world is not the essence of who we are. Regardless of our choices, there is a part of us which we cannot control, and which, in fact, makes things happen in our lives. We will ignore it as long as we can and when the pain finally becomes unbearable we will scream "Uncle." And then we must look in some shadowy areas inside of us to see what is living there.

At this point we acknowledge our unconscious Shadow: the storehouse for all those facets of ourselves which we have rejected, which we thought would lead us into danger, and which we tried to cut off and disown. If we could only dispose of anger, perhaps we thought, we would be more acceptable. Then others would love us and then we would be safe and then we would be happy and then life would be OK from that point on.

When we finally realize that playing our roles well—whatever role we have chosen to insure safety, whether it's Hard Worker, Compliant Companion, or Peacemaker—doesn't make life turn out "right," save us from our own pain, or make our struggles disappear, then we are taken aback, surprised. Our efforts don't work. We can't make this life turn out safely. We can't achieve harmony by willing it.

Now we realize we can't escape dealing with our own hidden monsters. The anger we tried to kill when we were four didn't die but has lived, hidden but growing in the dark parts inside of us. The vulnerability which we have tried so hard to deny by achieving competence in the adult world still exists. That little Child in so much pain is still in us, waiting to be picked up. We had hoped that she was gone but she waits for us. We can't walk away from our hurts. Finally, we give up trying to avoid them and decide to face them. At this moment of surrender we cry out and say, "I can't do it on my own. Is there anyone else out there?"

We may cry out in our churches or in our support groups or with friends or at work, but ultimately we are faced with looking into ourselves alone. We must confront those demons we haven't faced, so we sit down and slowly learn what our inner worlds are about. We learn to know ourselves in ways different from what we have known before. We realize that we are not who we would like to think we are. And we certainly are not who most other people think we are.

This journey inward is sometimes scary, but as we reunite with our forgotten parts, we experience an aliveness we haven't felt for a long time. We feel feelings we were afraid to feel and look at truths about ourselves we have been afraid to see. We find that as we acknowledge our feelings we can grieve for our disappointed hopes, our unsatisfied longings. Then we can let them go. By accepting our losses and allowing our inner voids to be felt, we allow the hurts in our unconscious to heal. We learn to trust the unconscious. It wants wholeness and health for us. It knows exactly what we need to have and to let go of. Through our unconscious, we find healing.

By moving through and healing our past pain, we are led into the realm of the collective unconscious, that part of the unconscious which joins us with everyone and everything else, forming a greater "whole." We notice that what happens to us in the external world mirrors what's happening within us. Conflicts within us are acted out outside of us. We acknowledge the mechanism of "projection"—seeing outside of ourselves what is happening inside.

Themes in our lives are repeated within and outside us. We may hear someone say what we have been thinking, or events coincide to create a desired solution without any effort on our part. The life process seems to be pulling us toward the wholeness which is specific for us. External rules lose their authority for us. We are guided from within, from some place deep in our bodies, not from our heads. All the different parts of us, our different voices are working together. Our energy is unified and focused. We may or may not put it into words, but we experience a sense of being taken care of, of being watched over, of being guided to those experiences which are perfect (if not easy) for us, in order to rectify any misperceptions and distortions. It is as though everything were drawing us to clarity.

When we feel this connection to the collective unconscious, we are moving into the "transpersonal" realm, that arena in which we deal with "ultimate values, unitive consciousness, . . . mystical experience, awe, being, self-actualization, essence, bliss, wonder, ultimate meaning, transcendence of the self, spirit, oneness, . . . and related concepts, experiences, and activities." (*Journal of Transpersonal Psychology*, vol. 1, p. 1, 1969.)

The search for this sense of unity is a difficult, uphill battle, because our culture denies both the personal and the collective unconscious, fostering extreme alienation from inner processes. Most of us deny that there is anything more to us than our minds and our bodies and we don't acknowledge our inner worlds. We deny our conflicts. We may find ourselves thinking: I want to be a loving person. I don't want to be angry all the time . . . but I am. Or: Why can't I be more efficient? These feelings won't go away and let me get my work done. Or: I have a beautiful home and family. Why aren't I happy? Too often we try to assuage these feelings with a kind of denial, refusing to acknowledge one part of us and becoming strongly identified with another part; a part we have learned is "acceptable." We try to will our lives to be as our minds tell us they should be.

Inevitably this denial of conflict causes individual stress which leads to family stress, which contributes to societal stress, resulting in global discord. What happens in our world only reflects our consciousness. The group consciousness cannot be higher or more peaceful than its component individuals' consciousnesses. While we are each responsible for our own inner worlds, very few people are aware of them or understand them.

One way to comprehend the workings of the unconscious inner world is to think in terms of subpersonalities. Subpersonalities do not indicate a split personality or psychosis. Subpersonalities are the different parts of us. We've always known about subpersonalities, we've just called them moods or roles or monsters. "It wasn't me who threw that plate; it was something crazy inside of me," we may say. Or, "Don't blame me, my devil made me do it."

Subpersonalities provide a way to structure our thinking and clearly describe different energies within us. We all know we have many sides to us. Some people develop one side of themselves, some another. But no matter which part of us is prominent at the time, we are still ourselves. There is an underlying ongoing consistency which we can identify as "I."

The fact that we can identify different parts of ourselves and feel the tension between them is a sign of health. Flexibility is the goal; we want to be able to move among our subpersonalities as the situation requires. We all have many, many subpersonalities. Over time new ones emerge and familiar ones mature.

Recently, I was preparing a seminar and I realized I needed to listen to my subpersonalities. I knew someone inside of me had something to say because I was feeling anxious. First I heard from the Wimp. She said, "You can't do this. You have nothing to offer. They'll hate you. It will be terrible." She offered these comments in a whining voice, a bit hysterically. Within a few minutes I heard from another female voice, the Hard Worker. She said, "Now, don't give in to that hysteria. Just look through every book on your bookshelf and gather all the information you need from others. Compile their quotes and build a presentation from that."

I started to follow the Hard Worker's direction. After an hour, I became frustrated and fatigued. Fatigue is another way I can tell I need to listen to some part inside of me. It indicates to me that one part has been dominant too long and others haven't been heard. When I sat back, I heard from the Masochist. She said, "Go ahead and suffer. It's only five more weeks. You can enjoy yourself later. Just forget about having fun next month." I found that rather depressing and went to bed.

The next morning, I was feeling refreshed. The first subpersonality I heard from was the Playful Child, a boy of about eight. He said that he wanted to have fun and he wanted the seminar to be fun. Several minutes later, I heard from the Creative Adult. This was another masculine voice, about thirty-four years old. He said, "Don't worry about breaking your back to get a lot of work done; just allow it to come from inside of you." He told me that I already knew everything I needed and to just pull from within me instead of gathering data from outside of me.

Over the next week, these five parts met together. I watched as the Creative Adult emerged as the leader of the group. He talked with each subpersonality individually and they agreed on the contribution each would make to the presentation. To the Wimp he said, "I appreciate your awareness that this seminar will take some preparation. You have reminded us that we can't disregard the work that needs to be done and put it off until the night before. Please keep reminding us every few days that we need to be preparing." To the Hard Worker he said, "I appreciate your sense of responsibility. I need you to make sure that the car is running well, that there is enough gas, and that you have precise directions to the location." The Hard Worker agreed and diligently assumed her duties. To the Masochist the Creative Adult said, "I appreciate your ability to persist. Please remind all of us that we need to work consistently on this project." She nodded and seriously contemplated her task. To the Playful Child he said, "I appreciate your enthusiasm. Please share that with the group. That would be a welcome contribution."

The Playful Child beamed, glad to be acknowledged. And for himself, the Creative Adult said that he would be responsible for the content of the presentation. He would create a seminar from his imagination and experience.

Each part agreed to do his or her appropriate task. I certainly didn't want the Masochist to be responsible for the content of the presentation or the Playful Child to be in charge of getting the directions and the car ready. Each subpersonality was satisfied to do a job appropriate for his or her characteristics.

We get into trouble when we expect one subpersonality to do a job which fits another subpersonality. When it's time to play, we need a Playful Child, and when it's time to work, we need a Responsible Adult. We also get into trouble when we give one subpersonality an inordinate amount of time and energy. If the Hard Worker is dominant ninety percent of the time, the other subpersonalities will feel stifled. If one subpersonality is disproportionately large, we are using our energy in an imbalanced way.

For those of us super-responsible, hard-working, long-suffering "good people," there is an imbalance in the time and energy we divide among our subpersonalities. We favor the Hard Worker or the Peacemaker and disregard the Selfish Child or the Sensuous Devil.

But now in adulthood we realize that we have to notice our other subpersonalities. We have had too many headaches and too much gastrointestinal disorder; we've been grinding our teeth too frequently and the insomnia is draining. So we look inside for the subpersonalities that are pressing for recognition. Now they won't wait any longer! They demand to be heard. So we must listen.

When I work with clients the first thing I do is listen to the different subpersonalities. In that way, we can define the conflicts and identify the unconscious beliefs underlying the client's feelings. It's easier for them to articulate the feeling that, "My Rebellious Teenager is angry and refuses to cooperate with my Compliant

Child" than it is for them to somehow analytically discern why they are always late even though they think they want to arrive on time.

When clients can differentiate the parts of themselves and speak clearly for each part, it's like turning on a light. Suddenly they recognize that the feelings of the Scared Infant are different from the desires of the Playful Child or the needs of the independence-seeking Adolescent.

Seeing clients go through this process of making sense of their inner world experience is exciting for me. They come to realize that they are not mixed-up, hysterical, insatiably needy people, but that there is a predictable order and logic to their behavior and their feelings. There are identifiable forces at work.

The subpersonalities in us are not static; they evolve. As their needs are met, they move into a new way of being. They grow up. All they need in order to mature is a nurturing environment. So when we give them what they need, they continue on their growing-up path. It's when they haven't received what they need that they remain stuck. It's then that they need to be listened to. Our inner worlds have their own standards and logic and operate consistently. They make sense in their own terms. When we know the unconscious, we understand what we need and how we react. Then we are no longer puzzling to ourselves.

As we attend to the needs of each subpersonality, the subpersonalities begin to cooperate. Each matures and a healthy integration of all the subpersonalities takes place. Our Reasonable, Compassionate Adult becomes stronger and more accessible to us.

The first step in this process of understanding your inner world is to just listen. Shift your focus inwardly and temporarily disregard the outer world with all of its activity and distraction. Take time to breathe, allow your mind to become quiet and experience a different way of being. The exercises at the end of each chapter are designed to put you in touch with your inner world. Doing the exercises will automatically communicate to your unconscious that you are open to discovering it. If you are truly open, your unconscious will make itself known.

Do you doubt this whole process? Skepticism is normal; it will not diminish the efficacy of the exercises. For the next month, do one of these exercises daily (they may be repeated, and you will begin to make up your own, as well) and write down your experiences. See if you notice patterns in your inner world that are reflected in your outer world. See what happens as you make a commitment to know and accept your inner life.

How to Use This Book

Each chapter in this book presents a case study followed by questions and imagery exercises which will put you in touch with your own subpersonalities. The first set of questions is meant to be answered immediately after reading the chapter. It is strongly advised that you do not put this off "for later."

The most effective way to do the imagery exercises is to tape record yourself (or a friend) reading them, and then sit back, relax and listen to the tape. A second set of questions, pertaining to the exercise, is provided to get you to think about your imagery experience.

You may find, at first, that you are not sure if you are doing the exercises "right." But there is no right way to do them. You may feel that your rational, thinking mind is getting in the way but, even if it feels like you are just "making it up," these images are also valuable and can teach you about yourself. The more you can relax, the more spontaneous your imagery will become. You may want to explore various relaxation methods—there are many books and tapes available on this topic. A basic relaxation script is provided on page 9.

The exercises may be repeated as often as you wish and will yield different results each time.

Good People 1

Like most of my clients, from some place way inside of me I've always had a longing to "be good." I've tried to figure out what the "right" thing in any given situation was and to do that. I've tried to be what I thought some authority wanted me to be.

Wanting to be good was a curse. Growing up in the sixties when the thing to do was to be cool, wanting to be good insured that I would never be quite "with it." No one else seemed to be burdened with that curse. I watched other kids having fun, doing crazy spontaneous things, not thinking too much about what they "should" do, just enjoying themselves.

Like my sister. She was one year younger than I, and always, growing up, she looked to me like the epitome of cool. She was popular and had lots of friends, dates and fun. She started trends while I couldn't even follow them. She knew all the new words and styles while mostly I thought about how awkward I must look to everyone. She was extroverted while I have always been painfully introverted. Was anything hard for her?

The only thing that wasn't hard for me was making good grades which resulted in further isolation from the other kids. But making good grades was one way of being good and getting loads of approval from my parents and teachers. Teachers always did think I was a good kid. I was sure I was doing what God wanted me to do when I got good grades. And I didn't have to work particularly hard for them. School was always an arena in which I could shine and experience success—sometimes the only arena.

The ultimate person to please was God. At the Catholic girls' school I attended, the structure for viewing reality was to follow God's rules as interpreted by the Sisters. Thus, it was ultimately pleasing to God if we were quiet when class started. God wanted me to avoid boys and to treat them as second class citizens if I ever had to speak to one of them. God didn't really like boys and didn't think too well of those people who did. So when I would snub Jimmy Thibadaux when he said hello, I knew I was pleasing God. If God were here, He would do the same thing. "Treat others as you would want to be treated" did not include boys, who were the source of evil and should be punished for having the bad taste to be born male.

Of course, understanding that much about boys, sex didn't need to be mentioned. If God didn't want you to talk to boys, you didn't need to ask about doing anything else with them. They were not to be treated with kindness.

Therefore, the implication was that I would be a better person and would be good in God's eyes if I were not sexual and didn't have sexual thoughts, feelings or interests. I didn't decide any of that consciously. My choice was so subtle and so deep that, without knowing it, the sexual part of me ceased to exist. And that was before it had really been born. So I never really had any sexual feelings or any physical desires. I did notice many years later that puberty was when I first started gaining weight and that around the time of my period, my appetite was always insatiable.

Eating too much or not exercising enough was never a sin or even a little bit wrong. If one were intellectual, the condition of the body was unimportant. In fact, being concerned about the body at all was discouraged. Having a body was one of the burdens related to being human and being relieved of that burden at death was definitely something to anticipate. Meanwhile, one should focus on developing a keen intellect and being as close to a pure spirit as is possible.

The amount of time kneeling in Church was indicative of the disrespect the Catholic Church seemed to have for bodies. Kneeling without resting one's derriere on the seat and keeping one's elbows off the railing was a discipline for the "weak body." If it pained a body, it was good. The discipline would get the body into line. With enough aching and with constant discipline, the spirit would learn to rise above the body and one would somehow end up a better person than before all the aching and discipline.

Saying "No" when the body said, "I'm uncomfortable and I'd like to move," would probably make God happy. If the body suffered, God was pleased. "No" was His favorite word.

God was a "He" in those days. Religion was a matter of denial and control, fraught with threats of punishment to be delivered by an angry, condemning male. Being good equalled always following the rules.

Discipline was a good way of silencing any voice that arose from inside. The inside of the body was not to be trusted, but to be disciplined and brought into line with the intellect, with doing what one "should." Nothing that would arise from inside my body, such as impulses, wishes, feelings or fantasies, would please God. God wanted a little nun—quiet, robot-like, doing things "perfectly."

I became obsessed with being perfect. Perfect meant having a non-threatening facade, fitting in and not making waves. Don't rock the boat. Be nice. Don't make anyone uncomfortable. Give people what they want. Be a pleaser. Don't think about your own wants.

And so, I learned not to trust my body, not to identify with it, not to even like it. It was not the source of anything "good." It was a long time before I was able to view these childhood concepts with any objectivity. But once I was able to do so, I knew that I wanted to help others examine their belief systems, and the pain those beliefs so often create.

❧ ❧ ❧ ❧ ❧

In my psychotherapy practice, the clients I talk with describe their life choices and decisions and express a desire to do the "right" thing. Each one is concerned with acting appropriately, being a participating member of society and doing her job well. Each one cares about making her life good, about enjoying being alive. They want their relationships to be satisfying, to have love given and received, and to feel comfortable and content.

When it comes time for a client to make a decision, to choose an action or to reconsider a position, she takes her responsibilities seriously. She thinks about what she has been taught is right, and she chooses to act in that way. When she was a child, a teacher or parent taught her that one behavior was "right" and another "wrong." This outer authority had credibility. The child trusted what she was told from outside of herself. Now as an adult in conflict, her first point of reference is always someone or something from the past, a former authority now alive in her head. She recalls some teaching or doctrine and applies that to herself in her current situation. Now she is "good," doing what she believes is expected.

These decisions usually result in continued pain for the client. The hope that her perseverance will finally result in situational change is often frustrated. Seldom are the rewards she expected for being good forthcoming. Life doesn't become easier, other people don't respect her more, relationships don't flourish.

Each client knows her own rules for being good and follows them, but her expectations about receiving protection from unhappiness as a reward for her efforts are unfulfilled. In fact, these people often hurt more, feel increased frustration and disappointment, and seem to be further from their goals of peace and happiness than before.

This process reinforces the client's perception of herself as a powerless child and someone else (parents, teachers, God) as a powerful authority. The authority has all the answers about how to make life work smoothly and the child has to guess the behavior expected of her in order to be taken care of by the authority.

By identifying with the powerless Child in themselves, these clients constantly guess answers which prolong their own pain, but which they hope "serve God" (whatever or whoever is the God in their lives). Fear is at the basis of their choices. They are suffering, but fear the consequences of not participating in their habitual patterns of interacting.

Perhaps always volunteering to chauffeur the school children is draining and frustrating but clients wanting to be "good" don't refuse. Perhaps living with a selfish, demanding husband is depleting, but "good" clients always continue to take care of him.

While growing up, these people didn't trust the voice which came from their own feelings or wants, but they did have another voice strongly implanted in their heads which was louder and demanded their compliance. Originally this voice came from outside of them, from a revered/feared authority. But after so much experience with that authority's expectations, the voice began to live within their heads. They could hear clearly and loudly just what the Authority expected even when they were alone.

That voice now has its own life within them. Other inner voices, the ones that are needy or wanting, are silenced in deference to this now internalized Authority. They believe the Authority voice will lead them to safety if they listen to it, while their wanting and needing voices will only lead them into danger. These Good People have opted out of their own feelings in favor of trusting an Authority whom they believe will keep them safe.

As children, they refused to accept the premise that safety was not possible, that pain would occur as part of life and feeling it could not be avoided. Thus, they sacrificed their own inner voices—their own wants, needs, feelings. When these inner voices weren't clearly heard any longer, the conflict between their own wants and what was expected of them wasn't clearly definable.

After years of living with family members who didn't acknowledge her wants, the client doesn't recognize her wants, either. After so much experience being the Selfless Giver, the client forgets that she needs to receive sometimes, too. The Authority voice received her allegiance and, consequently, grew louder. No other voice was acknowledged as consistently. And so the other voices grew softer until some were no longer heard at all.

Eventually, these Good People did not know when they felt fear or anger or fatigue or whatever else was the threatening "unacceptable" voice. That unacceptable part of them was no longer in evidence. There were no conflicts with the Authority. Any inner voices which did not comply with the Authority's expectations were silenced. Surely, a child must think, that's a small enough price to pay for love and protection. These early childhood beliefs continue throughout adulthood. But what worked in childhood to gain approval—being good and thinking of others—doesn't work in adulthood to bring satisfaction and contentment.

These Good People believe that they shouldn't be vulnerable. They shouldn't need what isn't easily forthcoming or want what they can't have. If they can't "solve" their own emotional conflicts in the outer world, they just won't have the feelings that cause so many problems. Needing to be self-reliant and in control means that they don't share their hurts and frustrations with another who might listen and sympathize and possibly offer another perception. Instead, they learn well to carry their suffering by themselves, accepting emotional isolation from others and from their own feelings. They side with the world outside rather than the world inside. They learn their roles well—whether at work or at home—about how they "should" behave. They fit in. They look perfect. (Except for the obesity or the compulsive dieting or the obsessive busyness.)

When Good People hurt, we say to ourselves, "Be quiet. Keep other people comfortable." When we are angry we say, "Don't make waves; do it their way." When we are needy, we say, "Think of all the folks who really have it bad. Don't be so selfish." For whatever voice arises from within us, we have a response to silence it. We ignore the power in our own feelings.

Part of us thinks that the only voice we need to hear is the one which tells us what we "should" do; but then we also develop insomnia, arthritis, migraines, constipation, colitis or obesity. And we may or may not put it all together that listening to that internalized Authority, while ignoring the inner feeling voices, results in physical pain for us. After all, who would think that just trying to be good would hurt your body?

Sound familiar? If you have ever thought in any of these ways or drawn any of these conclusions, I'd like to share my observations and experiences with you. Life hasn't been easy for me, and while I might like to point my finger at someone and say, "It's your fault; if you hadn't been around, I would have been happy," I know in my heart and soul that I can't avoid taking responsibility for myself that easily. Blaming is just a way of saying, "I don't want to look inside of me to understand how I am creating my own reality." As adults, we all do create our own realities to a great extent. Patterns do emerge in our lives at which we must look.

There is an undeniable correlation between our choices to ignore parts of our inner worlds, and our outer world experiences. If I disown some of my feelings, I will still see them but now they will look like they come from outside of me. It will appear that my husband is not sensitive to my feelings. In fact, however, he is just saying aloud what my inner subpersonality is already communicating.

Healing occurs when conflicts are resolved on an unconscious level. Healing demands that we re-own and integrate those parts of ourselves which have been alienated. Just because our parents ignored our Playful Child energy when we were young doesn't mean that, as adults, we can continue to ignore that part ourselves. It is ours.

Once we own these parts, we can come to know who is alive and operating within us. We may find that not only is there a Good Girl but also a Rebellious Teenager and an Angry Martyr. And probably they don't like each other! They certainly aren't working together for a common goal. You probably feel more comfortable with some subpersonalities than with others. You're probably willing to let your Loving Spouse or Gentle Parent be known, but you hesitate to let anyone see your Demanding Tyrant or your Selfish Materialist. Usually, we don't want to see the "unacceptable" parts ourselves. But they are alive and using our energy nevertheless. And their presence is certainly noticeable at times! So, if we want to listen to what *is*, we must open to whatever we hear and see from within us. It's a process of surrendering and allowing.

To begin this process, do the following relaxation. You may want to record these instructions on a tape recorder so that you can listen to them passively with your eyes closed. Or, have a friend with whom you feel comfortable read them to you.

Relaxation

Let yourself become comfortable. *(Pause for ten seconds.)* When you are ready, allow your eyes to close. *(Pause.)* For a few minutes follow your breathing, watching the air as it comes in and as it goes out. *(Pause.)* Let your mind be still and let the busyness of the day float away. Focusing your attention on your breathing, allow any thoughts to just pass through your mind as though they were dancers on a stage, entering from the left and leaving to the right. *(Pause.)* Follow your inhales and your exhales. *(Pause.)* Allow your breath to carry you deeper within yourself. *(Pause.)* Notice a slight letting go in your muscles and feel your body relax. *(Pause.)* Let yourself be drawn deeper within, allowing the outer world to fade away. All of your attention is focused on your inner world. *(Pause.)* Just follow your breathing. *(Pause.)* Allow yourself to be pulled deeper within.

The Control/Compliance Game 2

Wednesdays are quiet at the office; that's why I like them. Most of the other six therapists take the day off and leave their offices empty. Only Karen, whose office is in the corner, and I share the waiting room. I've arranged my schedule so that most of my work in the office is done on Wednesdays. It feels more "mine" then. I turn down the radio and close the outside door so there is very little noise intruding into my office.

I especially enjoy my time with my two o'clock client. Kate is forty-five and originally came into my office saying that she needed help letting go of her children. With her wavy red hair and hazel eyes, she sat alertly, not leaning against the back of the chair. She was neat and well groomed; no one could criticize her appearance unless it was for lack of flourish. By looking at her, I knew nothing about Kate except that she wanted to do everything "right." She did not present herself as someone who took risks.

Kate's sons were in their early twenties and had recently left home for graduate school. She sensed that her work in life would never be the same. For over twenty years Kate had listened and supported, providing warmth and acceptance for her family. She had lovingly created a home by caring about her husband and sons and sensitively responding to their needs. She had decorated and cooked and sewn and had truly enjoyed herself and her family. She was very proud of both her sons. She had loved her role of nurturing mother.

Kate described her relationship with Dan, her husband of twenty-five years, as unusually harmonious. They had always been especially close, sensing a tie they described as "lasting through many lifetimes." They had known each other from childhood and had married when Kate was twenty. They seldom argued and seemed to find an ongoing sense of appreciation and pleasure in each other's company.

Recently, however, Kate's significant relationships had altered. Her children no longer required her to be the nurturing mother. They were across the country and thinking about their own goals. She sensed, too, a change in her marriage relationship. Dan admitted that he was restless and was sensing his own shifts. He did not respond to her as compliantly as he had in the past. There were parts of him that pressed for greater expression and independence. Kate didn't resent these changes, but was left feeling confused and unsure about herself. She had always defined herself in terms of these three family relationships. Now it was time to "be" differently, and she didn't know what that meant or how to do it. She felt that she had lost most of what she had valued in her life until then, and was mourning her loss.

During our first meeting, Kate was pleasant but cried intermittently while talking. Her feelings were overwhelming but, more troubling to her, they were confusing. If she could understand what was happening to her, she said, she could handle it. At the end of our session, I realized that I had been touched by the depth of Kate's pain and by her confusion. "How could I be so unhappy," she seemed to be saying, "when I've always done everything I was supposed to do?"

Near the beginning of our second session I suggested that we do some imagery work. I surprised myself by doing this. Usually I wait several sessions until I sense that a trusting relationship has developed between the client and me. An unconscious part of me must have known that Kate would receive this suggestion openly. As I mentioned imagery, Kate's face brightened. She told me about a class that she and Dan had taken the previous year. They had learned that their imagery was spontaneous— totally separate from, and independent of, their conscious minds; arising from a source deep within them. In their class they had passively respected the integrity of their imagery, watching their mental pictures move and change spontaneously without any direction from their own minds or from another leader. Kate was comfortable working with imagery because of this prior experience.

In my work with clients, I don't usually explain imagery work in theoretical terms. I just say that we have all the wisdom we need inside of ourselves, in our unconscious minds, and our conscious minds can access that wisdom at any time. Imagery is the language of the unconscious. It communicates truths about ourselves to us. So, if there are apparent obstacles in our everyday conscious worlds, we can find the resources we need to move ahead by going inside to the unconscious.

When I do imagery work with clients, we both close our eyes and then I lead them into a state of deep relaxation for several minutes. We concentrate on watching the breath and allow our muscles to relax. We enter a realm of deeper consciousness in which the outer reality fades and is no longer the focus of attention. We move through the inner world, where a different way of being is called forth.

I often begin an imagery session by saying, "Sit comfortably in the chair. I will close my eyes and do this exercise with you." Then I talk them through a relaxation process similar to the one on page 9.

By walking with Kate through her imagery, I gain a glimpse of her inner world. I allow my mind to become blank and I follow her process. I have no sense of where we are going or what we will encounter. I don't want to guide her imagery journey in any specific way. My role is to facilitate her awareness of her unconscious. I know that her unconscious will guide us in the direction of growth and wholeness. I also know that neither my mind, nor Kate's mind, nor any other conscious intellectual process, could be so accurate or effective. So, during the initial relaxation, we both surrender to the process of the unconscious.

I have learned through my own experience that we can truly trust the unconscious. If we can understand its language —imagery—we can decipher its message. The unconscious message is unfailing in offering the precise guidance that's needed at the moment.

The many different energies we humans feel tend to express themselves within our minds as subpersonalities with voices. In recent years, more and more psychologists have been working with these inner voices, but many of them reduce the energies to the two that are easiest to recognize: the inner Parent and the inner Child. There is validity in this approach, but we humans are more complex than that. Our unconscious is rich and develops hundreds of detailed permutations of those two characters.

For example, we may have a part of us which pushes us to achieve, to acquire professional respectability—the Driver. The Driver may encourage us not to rest, demanding that we work toward our goals constantly. On Saturday afternoons, we may notice the prominence of the Lazy Layabout. And by Saturday night, another subpersonality has taken control of most of our energy, perhaps the Party Animal or the Flirt. One way to know the unconscious is to know the different subpersonalities operating within us.

In Kate's therapy, we relegate the conscious mind to the role of observer while the unconscious communicates with us in images about Kate's subpersonalities. Thus, Kate is often presented with pictorial representations of her subpersonality figures which she views passively, as though she were watching a movie. Sometimes she just "knows" what is happening between the subpersonalities and how they feel, and sometimes she "sees" a scene unfolding. It doesn't matter how Kate experiences her inner world, just that she is open to it. She allows it to come to her and guide her.

When Kate and I turn our attention inward, we often just wait for one subpersonality figure or another to emerge and to begin speaking. I guide Kate by saying, "Wait and listen. A figure from within you will appear to you. He or she has something to give you. Wait receptively. When an image becomes clear to you, describe it to me." Because of Kate's earlier experience with imagery, she can easily focus her attention within herself receptively and wait.

As Kate realizes which figure is coming to her she describes that figure's appearance, gender, age, and behavior. She sees the image unfold as she describes it to me and sometimes laughs or cries as the figure says something to her. It is a revelation for her, as though she is watching a play she has no part in producing. In fact, her unconscious mind is delivering the images to her and her conscious mind is remaining quiet in order to receive them.

I follow along with my own imagery, visualizing what she describes. I often ask her to ask the figure in her mind a question. After doing so, she tells me how that figure responded. Kate varies her imagery sessions, sometimes carrying on conversations with her internal figures, and sometimes just watching their activity and reporting it to me as it unfolds. Her imagery has a spontaneity of its own and Kate is comfortable allowing her mind to watch it and report it.

Kate's ability to relax her intellectual control enough to hear from her inner voices is a sign of strength. She is comfortable acknowledging her imagery figures within the context of therapy. She doesn't feel overrun by them.

One of the first parts of Kate whom we met was a very young, playful male—the Little Rascal. (His name "came" to her as his image appeared.) He was full of fun. He would hide and jump and play pranks. There was nothing serious about him.

The Little Rascal was not intimidated by anyone, not even her Judge, a large stern female figure behind a huge desk who would give Kate her "shoulds." The Judge would be reprimanding the Little Rascal or giving him a job to do and he would tease her. He loved puns and enjoyed turning the Judge's words into a joke. Although he often didn't make a dent in her severe demeanor, neither did he let her commands ruin his fun.

After several weeks, Kate could say that the Little Rascal provided her with a moderating influence. When Kate took herself too seriously, he would make fun of her. When she was overburdened by responsibilities, he would laugh. He was gentle with her but always showed her a creative way of viewing herself in her situation. He introduced humor and reminded her repeatedly, "Practice, practice, practice enjoying yourself." "He's like a breath of fresh air," she would say.

Kate also met the Reader, a female figure about sixteen years old who was quiet and generally didn't interact with people. Mostly, she stayed by herself and read. She didn't want to make trouble. The Reader was closely related to a figure we soon learned was prominent with Kate, the Dutiful Daughter. Kate imaged the Dutiful Daughter as a slender, twenty-year-old woman with long, straight brown hair. She was timid and self-effacing. The Dutiful Daughter wanted the approval of everyone, particularly the Judge. The Dutiful Daughter decided what she would do based upon knowing what the Judge expected of her. Just as the Little Rascal was all spontaneity, the Dutiful Daughter had no spontaneity, only duty. She seemed to view herself as powerless and her only role to be that of pleasing the Judge.

Kate soon realized that most of the time she was identified with the Dutiful Daughter subpersonality. She reacted to others and spoke in the same manner that the Dutiful Daughter reacted and spoke. By identifying with the Dutiful Daughter, Kate blocked out her spontaneity (the Little Rascal contained all of that) and her own authority over herself (the Dutiful Daughter was focused on the *Judge's* authority). She became submissive, fearful, and strove to accomplish the impossible goal of making the Judge happy. And that's how Kate lived most of the time.

By identifying with the Dutiful Daughter subpersonality, Kate lived with fear and frustration. She was aware of that tension—of her anxiety and her desire to please. Kate could describe and consciously own her Dutiful Daughter qualities. She would tell me that she liked to be helpful and compliant.

The Judge was a subpersonality with whom Kate was not so consciously identified. Although Kate generally did not present herself to others as a Judge, the Judge aspect of Kate was evident to her family. They were familiar with her subtle criticisms about what was not acceptable, her pursed lips when she was dissatisfied, her raised eyebrows and averted eyes when she was angry. Kate didn't want to see her own rigidity and didn't want to be seen by others as "controlling." She found these qualities distasteful and so, she denied having them. This refusal to become conscious of the Judge-like part of her only fueled the Judge, giving it power and influence, and making it inevitable that its qualities would emerge in Kate's interactions with others from time to time.

On a very subtle level, the Dutiful Daughter understood the Judge's commands and immediately tensed to respond to them. Yet, because Kate was not well acquainted with the Judge, she didn't identify with being the one who caused the Dutiful Daughter pain, she only identified with the recipient of the pain. In the Judge/Dutiful Daughter polarity, Kate owned the Dutiful Daughter qualities consciously, and expressed the Judge qualities unconsciously.

Kate also recognized another subpersonality whom she called Mark Twain. Mark Twain was especially good at giving Kate advice about being grounded and stable. He had common sense and was reasonable. He had no need to please and didn't acknowledge other subpersonalities as having any authority over him. His frequent statement to Kate was, "Trust yourself." This subpersonality represented a confident, Adult part of Kate.

Obviously, Mark Twain wasn't a subpersonality with whom Kate identified easily, as she did with the Dutiful Daughter. Over time, she came to learn that he was an available resource within her whom she could trust. She contacted Mark when she wanted to and he responded to her needs. He never imposed himself on her. His wisdom was subtle, but Kate recognized his fairness and his integrity. She felt confident when she acknowledged him.

By listening to, questioning and watching her inner selves for several months, Kate learned that she was tyrannically ruled by the Judge, who would never be satisfied. She saw that she was usually trapped by her identification with the Dutiful Daughter, who would never stop trying to please the Judge. Into these scenes of female figures she might introduce the masculine flavor of Mark Twain or the Little Rascal. I would suggest to Kate, "See Mark Twain magically appear out of the shadows. He has a message for the Dutiful Daughter. Listen. Hear what he says to her."

Or I might say, "Let's see what the Little Rascal would do in this scene. Notice him entering the picture and tell me what happens."

Often Kate would sense a release of tension when one of the males appeared. The Little Rascal added humor and Mark added detachment. Just by the introduction of these two masculine figures, the tone of many of the discussions between the Dutiful Daughter and the Judge was altered. Kate imaged the feminine figures to have characteristics which were closer to her awareness—compliance, orderliness, respect. Her masculine figures owned those characteristics which Kate hadn't yet integrated into her daily way of being—self-confidence, assertiveness, playfulness, independence. All of her subpersonalities belonged to her; some were just easier for Kate to identify with.

Kate could consciously say she wanted to be liked (Dutiful Daughter). After much hard work in therapy, she realized that she (the Judge) was pressuring herself (the Dutiful Daughter) to meet traditional cultural expectations to earn approval. When she could laugh at herself for taking these "shoulds" so seriously (Little Rascal), she could view herself objectively (Mark Twain). Thus, her subpersonalities could balance each other.

But Kate's Judge had a strong grip on her. Sometimes Kate would describe a pain in her shoulder or a tightness in her chest. During the imagery when she would focus on her body experience, she would spontaneously visualize a fist squeezing her, trying to cut off her breath, if it grabbed her in the chest; or trying to break her resistance to its control if it tightened her shoulder. When she described the Judge, her voice would become softer as though she were intimidated by an external threatening figure. Her fear of the Judge's control was deep.

Several times Kate mentioned the word "power" as describing personal effectiveness. She quickly admitted that she was afraid of her own power. She knew the Judge did not want her to have a sense of her own power and also realized that the Dutiful Daughter resisted being powerful. When we spoke before the imagery sessions, she would express fear that owning her power and acting powerfully would alienate others from her and would deprive her of her connections to love. The Judge had told Kate adamantly that if she (Kate) relinquished a pleasing facade, no one would want to be around her. The Dutiful Daughter believed this statement completely.

All of her life, while she had not been aware consciously of this message, Kate had acted in accordance with it. She was a Peacemaker in groups, a Reliable Worker on the job. She mentioned that she and Dan had most wanted to teach their children not to intrude on others, never to be resented. This was certainly Kate's rule for herself. All of her relationships had been structured, unconsciously, on this basis. She was ready to serve others and never made requests which would leave anyone uncomfortable.

As she told me about her rules for herself, she expressed no conflict. "I was raised to be a good Catholic girl," she said, and she was consciously maintaining that role. She also expected appreciation for this from others. When she was not adequately appreciated, she felt resentful and used, but she never changed her behavior. Only the three people in her family saw her Shadow side, that darker world where she shoved her anger, power, and vulnerability.

The Shadow is the unconscious receptacle for those parts of us we deem "unacceptable." Kate's Shadow received any characteristic her Judge condemned. Since the Dutiful Daughter was obedient, her Shadow contained her rebellion; her Dutiful Daughter was sweet, but her Shadow housed her rage. Kate's controlling Judge didn't want the Dutiful Daughter to acknowledge her anger, fear, or need to be assertive, and didn't want the world to see these things, either. The Dutiful Daughter feared the possible consequences of disapproval or rejection or abandonment from other people if they did see these parts of her. (Kate's family didn't really count as being "other people" to Kate; consequently, their acceptance of her Shadow side didn't really count. By discounting the fact that her family loved her even though they had seen her Shadow, Kate held onto her belief that she would be rejected if her Shadow side were known.)

Kate reported having difficulty sleeping and severe tension headaches at times. When I suggested that there might be a correlation between her Dutiful Daughter role and these physical complaints, she became very innocent. We had learned that when Kate didn't want to see something unacceptable within herself, she would adopt an attitude of, "Oh, well, lots of people have trouble. I can live with it." This willingness to tolerate suffering was preferable to realizing that she wasn't innocent, that she did have a dark side, and that there did exist within her feelings which didn't fit with "a good Catholic girl" image.

The Judge was a controlling part of Kate who demanded that Kate be good. The Judge defined good as always being nice, never confronting anyone with any kind of need, giving others what they wanted, doing as she was expected to do, and, essentially, being invisible. Kate was not to listen to her own feelings, but only to the Judge telling her what she should do or should feel or should want.

Kate had lived according to the Judge's commands for most of her life until she entered therapy. She was convinced that she didn't feel anger or resentment. She believed that she liked being the one others depended upon and that maintaining any relationship at all required that she be strong, good, and not needy.

So, Kate had unconsciously resolved any conflict between her feelings and the controlling Judge's commands by not having any unacceptable feelings. Without her conscious mind having to think about it, her anger, fear and vulnerability were repressed into her unconscious and became part of her Shadow. They didn't cease to exist, but they ceased to be noticeable. They were alive but hidden. Her repression of those parts of her kept her safe from the Judge's punishment. There was no conscious decision to be made. She just didn't have unacceptable feelings. She did, though, have insomnia and headaches, but that kind of suffering was better than incurring punishment from the Judge. Her Dutiful Daughter was terrified of any confrontation with the Judge.

When Kate had stated that she was afraid of her personal power, she was saying that the Judge had told her that any "selfish," personally powerful part of her was bad. The Dutiful Daughter was afraid of being bad, feeling her own feelings, and thereby incurring the Judge's punishment. (Therefore, any feeling which came from inside of Kate had to be screened, and perhaps, censored.) But in expressing fear of her personal power, Kate was also expressing her fear of the intensity of her buried resentment. So many years of identifying with the Dutiful Daughter, bowing to the Judge's commands and ignoring wants from her other subpersonalities left her with repressed anger. Subpersonalities can't be ignored or denied without consequences. Kate must have unconsciously had a sense of the undercover conflict which was raging within her between her Judge's need to control and her rebellious feelings.

Although her Judge's will seemed to govern, her Shadow subpersonalities' wants and needs (for relaxation and unrestricted expression of feeling) never disappeared. They were only repressed so that she wasn't aware of them, but they were still very much alive. As with anyone whose voice isn't acknowledged, her anger grew. Repression requires ongoing energy to maintain the unnatural equilibrium.

Kate feared the disruption of this equilibrium and the expression of her unacceptable feelings. Certainly if her feelings were not controlled, she would not live up to the Judge's expectations that she be good. What would happen then if the Judge were dissatisfied with her, and if everyone else left her, as the Judge predicted they would, because she let her feelings show? That was too great a risk to take.

So, always, the decision (unconsciously) was to stuff her anger, her wants and her fears, and to continue acting in her very controlled manner. Thus, the insomnia and headaches continued. Her anger and her needs didn't disappear; they only changed shape. Physical symptoms were more acceptable to have than "ugly" feelings.

Kate and I spoke about personal power/effectiveness for several sessions and always experienced the total control of the Judge vetoing it. We seemed to hit a concrete wall. At this point Kate would back off and "resolve" her conflict about assuming her own power by denying it. The Dutiful Daughter would again dominate and the insomnia continued.

One session, Kate mentioned that she thought there were additional subpersonalities within her whom she didn't know. She didn't have an Adult personality who was comfortable, relaxed, spontaneous. (This was how she wanted to live when she grew up. Life was still unfolding. This wasn't it. Her real life would start later.) Without using imagery, I asked her to tell me her first association with being relaxed and spontaneous. What would she need to be that way? She immediately heard inside of herself, "For your mother to die." That didn't feel to me like a statement of physical fact, so I wanted to find the Mother part of Kate who was oppressing her.

In her imagery that day, we were taken to another world peopled with figures in bright clothing. She saw her real mother and her son walking toward her, each wanting to give her something heavy to carry. She realized that she didn't want to carry their burdens, but that her feet were in concrete boots attached to the earth so that she couldn't walk away. She noticed the muscles in her stomach and shoulders tighten. She thought that perhaps this would offer her a shield to forestall the two approaching figures. They didn't notice the shield, however, and kept approaching. Kate felt no way to defend herself against what she perceived as an unwelcome intrusion.

Then her imagery shifted suddenly. She was in a steaming cauldron being stirred by a huge paddle. Holding the paddle was a Witch dressed in a black robe. (Kate had noticed that the Judge was always in black and the Dutiful Daughter always in white—no gray, no in-between.) I instructed her to raise herself directly out of the cauldron, turn her back on the Witch, and float away. She said that when she raised herself out of the cauldron, she saw someone else in there and the Witch was continuing to stir. She was unwilling to leave the scene and allow this other person to remain in the cauldron.

At this point Kate was in tears. She was confronting her possible alternatives—to continue in her role as the recipient of the Judge/Witch's oppressive whims or to cut her ties to that way of relating. She felt overwhelming guilt about leaving the scene. To myself, I interpreted her wanting to rescue the new figure in the cauldron as still wanting to interact with the Judge, still trying to change her, not wanting to let go of that relationship. Some part of Kate still had hope that she could make it "turn out right."

The Witch/Judge part of Kate ruled her. Its voice sounded like an external, fear-inspiring, punitive authority, not just another voice among the group of her inner voices.

Kate recognized the imbalance that her fear of the Witch/Judge reflected. If her Dutiful Daughter shrank from contact with the Witch/Judge, she knew she needed to call on another subpersonality. She wanted a subpersonality who wasn't easily intimidated to move her inner process forward.

Kate wrote in her journal at this time:

> I can't force any changes on the Judge/Witch and I can't will her to disappear. She's a part of me and will always be with me in some form. I need to form a relationship with her. (The thought of asking her to talk to me is scary, but the less I know about her, about what she is feeling and thinking, the more impact she has on me. She can really beat me up if I ignore her. That scares me more!)

Kate then recorded what she observed in an imagery session:

> I needed a subpersonality who wasn't afraid of the Judge to form a relationship with her. So I called on Mark Twain. He asked the Judge to tell us about her childhood. (That seemed less scary.) She showed me an image of a pretty six-year-old girl with blonde curls and a pink ribbon. The girl was standing with her toes behind a line that was painted on the floor. The little girl wanted very much to step over the line but feared the severe punishment which she knew would follow. The girl decided to be good, not to cross the line. She decided to become a proponent of those rules which restricted her instead of being the one restricted. (This kid wasn't going to be a Victim!) She became "steely" inside so that she wouldn't feel her own disappointment about not venturing beyond her limits. She grew up relating to the world in a legalistic manner, not allowing gentleness or softness in her. The Judge grew into an adult with no close relationships and no one with whom she could share her conflicting feelings.

In our next therapy session, Kate asked Mark Twain to take the Judge back to the time in her childhood when the girl made the decision to be a Judge. At that point we played an alternative "tape." Kate viewed the scene in which the girl wanted to step across the line. I suggested, "This time the scene will develop differently. Put no effort into it, just watch and see what happens." Spontaneously, Kate saw a much larger figure place hands on the girl's shoulders, letting the girl know that the action of stepping across the line would be acceptable. The girl proceeded and explored beyond the line, knowing that she was protected. The girl walked with confidence and comfort.

Kate followed the growth of that girl into adulthood and old age in her imagery. This time the figure developed into an Earth Mother rather than a Judge. This Earth Mother was a nurturing, spiritual teacher. Kate described her as a large, older woman dressed in a loose caftan. Her skin was dark and worn and her expression was gentle.

I asked Kate to receive some words from this Earth Mother for the Judge. The Earth Mother softly told the Judge to rest. She suggested that the Judge use her cloak to wrap around her and that she hide herself in that cocoon. I instructed the Judge to go into that cocoon for thirty seconds which would be the equivalent of a four month vacation. She did so and Kate and I breathed deeply while Kate watched the Judge in the cocoon.

After many seconds, Kate saw a bolt of lightning over the cocoon. Intuitively, Kate realized that the lightning was a supernatural infusion, releasing the Judge from her self-control. The rigid shell around the Judge fell away. The tension released and Kate could see that the Judge was transformed. She emerged from the cocoon in a white and gold robe. Her manner was peaceful. She stated that her power would now be used for enrichment, not control.

Kate cried quietly for a few minutes. She had truly felt the shift in her Judge and the release of the rigidity containing the old hurts and disappointments. There had been an opening, a letting go of fears, and a rush of aliveness. The Judge emerged from the cocoon resembling the Earth Mother.

Kate had watched these images unfold and had listened to the words spoken. She hadn't directed the imagery, but had allowed it to be and to guide her into a relationship with her Judge. She respected the life of her inner world and the integrity of the Judge. The Dutiful Daughter was afraid of the Judge, but Kate was committed to working out a relationship between them.

The Earth Mother acknowledged the Dutiful Daughter's fear and saw her hidden anger. Because the Earth Mother could accept that the Dutiful Daughter was wounded and in pain behind her apparent compliance, she could help her to heal. The Earth Mother told the Dutiful Daughter to write about her resentments over the years toward the Judge. Kate allowed the Dutiful Daughter subpersonality to dominate and recorded her thoughts in her journal:

> I resent that you (the Judge) have made me detach from my feelings of loneliness, anger, helplessness; that you never cared about me enough to talk with me or to listen to me; that you only wanted to shout orders at me; that you only gave me rules, not any part of yourself; that you were always so busy "doing" a project that you never had time just to be with me; that you laughed at my feelings; that you criticized my feelings; that you were cruel to me when I needed you to protect me; that everything was pretense for everyone else's benefit, nothing was sincere; that you were so controlling; and that you never apologized to me for hurting me.

Then the Earth Mother told the Dutiful Daughter to imagine that she spoke these words to the Judge and that the latter figure acknowledged them. In her imagery Kate heard the Judge from her past reply, "Yes, I understand what you're saying, but I am the way I am." Then the Dutiful Daughter truly saw the Judge as a person separate from herself. And when she understood that this former authority figure was the way she was because that was just her way and not because she, the Dutiful Daughter, was inadequate, she sighed and released her. Their old game of Control/Compliance was no longer interesting. The Dutiful Daughter didn't need to participate in that game any longer. She saw the Judge from her past objectively and realized that she could react by *not reacting*.

Over the next weeks Kate wrote:

> As I watched the Dutiful Daughter detach from the Judge, I felt a release of her anger. There was nothing left to resist or to please,

there was no game, thus no hope of winning or fear of losing. The Dutiful Daughter just walked away from the Judge. She had felt acceptance and support from the Earth Mother without having to perform to receive it. She had felt grounded and confirmed, thus more secure. Now, when I sense her presence, I can't call her the Dutiful Daughter. Her "duty" sprang from fear and that's not her motivating energy anymore. She seems older, wiser and calmer. Through her, I had tried very hard, to my detriment usually, to gain from the Judge what the Earth Mother lovingly and freely gave. And now there seems to be an integration. The Earth Mother and the Dutiful Daughter have blended in a comfortable way. I feel more at home inside myself, less like I'm searching for something, less restless. I'm listening and responding to my feelings on an hourly basis now. Oh, yes, and last night I dreamt that my mother had died and that I placed flowers on her grave. I loved her but she was gone.

By letting go of her participation in the Control/Compliance game, Kate allowed the oppressive inner Authority to die. Without the support from her Earth Mother, Kate could not have taken the risks necessary to do this. She trusted her subpersonalities to guide her beyond the impasse and followed their direction. A resolution emerged which she couldn't have consciously chosen.

Just as the Earth Mother attended to the Dutiful Daughter's needs, she also attended to the Judge. The Judge was originally a healthy subpersonality in Kate who had gotten on a track of being a Controller to prevent pain and to gain approval. Kate, as a child, had feared punishment so much that she developed an inner voice, the Judge, who would tell her when she was nearing danger (an external authority's anger). Then the Judge would tell her to withdraw and be "nice."

Because this system for being safe in the world worked so well in Kate's younger life—her parents and teachers said she never caused problems—the Judge was given more and more of Kate's energy. Over the years, the Judge's dominance increased until Kate felt tyrannized from within. Her original goal of staying safe from others' retribution had indeed been met. In fact, the Judge had been so effective in doing that, that without realizing it, Kate had relied upon her more and more. Most of Kate's energy finally was taken by the Judge.

With help from Kate's other subpersonalities, particularly the Earth Mother, Kate could realign her energy. Kate understood that the Judge was using her strength to keep Kate safe as Kate had at one time asked her to do. When she realized that her own childhood longing for love was behind the Judge's rigid behavior, Kate could allow the Judge to relax her rigid defense. The Earth Mother in Kate had all the love Kate needed, but the Dutiful Daughter's fear had been blocking that love by sapping all of Kate's energy.

Kate had to care about her Judge and pay attention to her for this realignment to happen. The Judge didn't change because she was hated or pressured. **Just like people, subpersonalities grow and develop with attention and nurturing.** After many months of work, Kate had gained enough distance from her unconscious identification with the Dutiful Daughter to adequately *observe* the Judge, not identify with her or become her Victim. Mark Twain was helpful in strengthening Kate's detachment and ability to observe. Kate was, thus, willing for a true intimacy to develop between the Earth Mother and the Judge.

In Kate's childhood, she had thought that she would receive acceptance only for some parts of her—her compliance, sweetness, and helpfulness, i.e., her Dutiful Daughter qualities. But behind her Dutiful Daughter facade, her "less acceptable" feelings lived. Her Dutiful Daughter's fear was so strong that she was unable to relate to the Judge in any way that was not fear based. So Kate needed Mark Twain's objective understanding of the Judge.

After learning about the childhood fear behind the Judge's harsh words, Kate could treat the Judge compassionately. By recognizing the Judge's motivation to earn love, Kate could forgive her for her seemingly uncaring ways and nurture the Judge's need for understanding. By accepting the Judge's feelings, Kate could be patient as the Child/Judge grew up.

The Judge was a childhood concept of what being good was. As this figure grew up and her hidden vulnerability was treated gently, she developed with gentleness. As she grew up, the Judge learned to value relationships, not control. When she no longer had to deny her needs, the Judge did not prohibit Kate's other subpersonalities from meeting their needs. No longer did she try to curtail the Little Rascal's fun or criticize the Dutiful Daughter's assertiveness.

As Kate related to the feelings behind the Judge's stern demeanor, she saw that what she had thought was the Judge, was really just a Child trying to act grown-up, to be strong and not fearful, in the only way she knew. As Kate helped the Child mature, by accepting her and listening to her, the Child developed into a strong, nurturing, loving Adult.

Her inner wounds may have originated in childhood, but her inner selves had been interacting for years in ways that perpetuated this pain. With the influence of Mark Twain's detachment and the Earth Mother's nurturance, the subpersonalities could interact differently. With the Earth Mother's support, the Dutiful Daughter was no longer confronted with the possibility of dying (her fear of the result of abandonment by the Judge). So, when the Judge demanded, "Don't feel anything, or else!" Kate/Dutiful Daughter could ignore the command. As Kate wrote:

> Or else what? The Judge won't approve of me? Who cares? I have the Earth Mother with me. She loves, accepts and supports me and she really knows me! She knows me better than anyone ever has and she still wants me around! Knowing she's on my side gives me confidence. I don't need the Judge. I don't hate the Judge, either. We colluded for a long time, but I'm not playing that game anymore.

Thus, both the Judge and the Dutiful Daughter evolved and matured, each accepting the other as each had her own needs met.

Kate was first wounded in her childhood when she was dependent on external authorities' approval. But by her natural assumption of her roles to aid her in interpreting her experience and protecting herself, she maintained an inner imbalance which prevented healing. It was her challenge to confront this inner energy imbalance and to correct it. By acknowledging that she was responsible for continuing her own woundedness through the dysfunctional interactions among her subpersonalities, Kate also implicitly acknowledged her responsibility for healing those interactions. If she could maintain imbalance, she could maintain balance! By her willingness to detach from and observe her usual patterns of interaction among her subpersonalities (that is, by not identifying with the Dutiful Daughter and the Judge, but by employing Mark Twain's detachment), she could notice her other subpersonalities and acknowledge their wants. No longer was there a feared Shadow, unable to be integrated or trusted.

With the information gathered by Mark Twain, the Earth Mother was able to nurture the Judge. By caring in this very basic way and relating to her Judge, Kate had experienced a transformation of the Judge. She had acknowledged the Judge's autonomy and realness and respected that. She didn't try to ignore the Judge or to overpower her. She just acknowledged her existence and accepted her right to be the way she was. Therefore, the previously disowned feelings were welcomed back, felt, and made a part of Kate's awareness of herself.

Kate couldn't disregard her responsibility to integrate her other subpersonalities into her life, nor could she ignore the Judge. By listening to the wants of all the subpersonalities instead of allowing only one part to make decisions, Kate encouraged her subpersonalities to evolve. The attempt to deal with feelings by denying them was abandoned in favor of maintaining communication among all her subpersonalities. Just by keeping conversation open, unexpected resolutions emerged.

Kate experienced a vitality she hadn't felt before. No longer did she know what she would do in every situation. Now she could be surprised and delighted by the unfolding guidance presented to her from within. As her subpersonalities lived peacefully together and felt nurtured in their needs, Kate sensed a growing aliveness and creativity in herself. Living her life with the participation of all her subpersonalities became an alternative she enjoyed. She no longer responded out of fear, but out of the joy and spontaneity which is natural for healthy subpersonalities. Her relationships with her husband and children reflected her inner ease. They shared a deeper level of intimacy, based on respect for each person's individuality.

Are you thinking, "Well, that's fine and good for Kate, but I don't see people who aren't there, and I definitely don't hear voices." Come on now. Don't you know what your mother would say about that deal you made last week? About the way you talked with your friend? About that encounter which left you so uncomfortable? You know your mother so well that she doesn't even have to be around for you to know what she would say. There is a part of you that is like a little Mother, whispering (or yelling) at you, telling you to "Be sweet" or "Don't make waves" or whatever was your mother's favorite expression. There's a voice inside that says that to you all the time, right?

What was your mother's (and now your internal mother's) most frequent message to you?

_____
_____
_____
_____

And your father? Maybe he didn't put his wishes into words (or maybe he did), but you received messages from him about how he wanted you to be. What was his most frequent message?

_____
_____
_____
_____
_____
_____
_____

Just by watching how your father acted, you learned something about how to be. What did you learn?

_____
_____
_____
_____
_____
_____
_____
_____
_____

By watching your mother, what did you learn about how to be?

_____
_____
_____
_____
_____
_____
_____
_____

How was that learning taken inside of you and made part of who you are today?

_____
_____
_____
_____
_____
_____
_____
_____
_____

So, you can understand how significant people from your early life are still living with you in your own subpersonalities. You don't need to blame anyone from your past. Your Parent or Judge or Witch subpersonality is alive now and s/he's all yours! You got your clues from what you thought you saw with your real mother, but now your internalized Mother is yours. She speaks to you and you relate to her.

How do you relate to that Mother in you?

_____
_____
_____
_____
_____
_____
_____
_____
_____
_____

Do you fear her?

Do you resent the way she controls you?

What does that internalized Mother say to you (probably very subtly) to control your behavior?

Do you like her strength?

When you are strong, what part of that strength comes from her?

In which of your behaviors do you notice your Father subpersonality?

How would you describe your Father subpersonality?

What is his outstanding characteristic?

Do you fear him?

Do you resent his control?

What does the internalized Father subpersonality say to you to control your behavior?

_____
_____
_____
_____
_____
_____

Do you like his strength?

_____

When you are strong, what part of that strength comes from him?

_____
_____
_____
_____
_____
_____

How much of your time and energy does your Father subpersonality receive?

_____
_____
_____
_____
_____

How do your Mother and Father subpersonalities relate to each other inside you?

How and when do they conflict?

How and when do they cooperate?

In comparison, which subpersonality is stronger?

Who has the louder voice?

Who influences your choices about work?

About friends?

Let's do the same thing Kate did to contact her inner world figures. First, do the relaxation exercise on page 9. (Or, if you already have your own special way of relaxing, do that now.) Then do the following exercise. (Again, it helps to record these instructions so that you may listen to them passively with your eyes closed.)

Exercise

Allow an image to come to you of you walking. Just wait receptively until it comes to you. *(Pause for thirty seconds.)* Where are you? Notice the details of your surroundings. Look all around you. *(Pause.)* Are you inside or outside? *(Pause.)* Now imagine the scene as though you were a bird and you were looking down on it. Which subpersonality do you see? *(Pause.)* If you are not sure of the name or label for the subpersonality ask him/her. What do you hear? *(Pause.)* Notice how that part of you moves. Does s/he walk smoothly and easily? *(Pause.)* Is s/he carrying something? *(Pause.)* Just from seeing the body posture, how would you guess this figure feels? *(Pause.)* Keep following this figure as s/he walks. S/he comes to a break in the walkway, perhaps a stream if s/he is outside, or a wall if inside. What does the figure do? What seems to be his/her response to an obstacle? Just watch and notice what happens next. *(Pause for three minutes.)*

Describe your imagery experience:

You may have noticed that while you were doing the exercise, you could let go of intellectual control and watch the scene unfold. Or was it a struggle for you not to be in charge of the action? Could you allow yourself to be passive?

_____
_____
_____
_____

What happened at the obstacle?

_____
_____
_____
_____
_____
_____

How is this characteristic of what happens in your life?

_____
_____
_____
_____
_____
_____

What subpersonality reacts when you're frustrated? How does it react?

_____
_____
_____

_____

_____
_____
_____
_____
_____
_____
_____

What part of you tells you how you "should" be?

_____
_____
_____
_____
_____

Allow yourself to relax, breathe deeply, and wait. An image of that figure that gives you your "shoulds" will come to you. Wait receptively until you see that figure. *(Pause.)* What do you notice about that figure's clothing?

_____
_____
_____
_____
_____

What do you notice about his/her behavior?

_____
_____
_____
_____
_____

Just by being in front of you, without using words, what message is that figure communicating?

What reaction do you notice in your own body as it receives that message?

What feelings do you feel?

Just let whatever is there be there, and keep breathing. Use this space to write down any additional feelings you have about the exercise or your responses.

Our Lives are Projections 3

The patterns in our significant relationships reflect the way we treat ourselves. It's not possible to construct an outer reality which does not mirror the inner reality. They are two landscapes—one visible and one invisible, but both the same. Often we have masked the inner landscape with illusions, hopes and distortions, but the projection of our inner world onto the outer world never lies.

Projection involves seeing outside of you a manifestation of what exists inside of you. If I meet a woman whose husband continually abuses her and she chooses to stay with him, I know that some subpersonality inside of her doesn't nurture her feelings and needs. He acts out what exists within her. On an unconscious level, one of her subpersonalities believes another deserves abuse. She projects the abusive subpersonality while identifying with and acting out the abused Victim.

It really isn't possible to feel unworthy and to have others treat you as being worthy and valuable to them. Usually you will find another who will treat you exactly the way you (unconsciously) believe you deserve to be treated. It would be nice, wouldn't it, if our experience with others would offer some respite from the constant tearing down within our heads which we do to ourselves. But it seldom happens.

The unconscious is responsible for creating these projections in the outer world. We certainly wouldn't will some of the things which happen to us, but for anything which occurs, we need to consider: how have I contributed to making this situation exist? It's like having an unseen light illuminate the shadowy recesses within us and then project them onto a movie set for us to walk through. What we see around us is already operating within us. But it's so much easier to view when it's acted out around us by our family, friends, colleagues and acquaintances. They don't know they're following our script, but they treat us exactly the way some subpersonality inside treats us. They're just easier to see. (And we're doing the same thing for them. We mirror some subpersonality and they react to us the way they react to that inner part of themselves.)

Our unconscious subpersonalities often want very different experiences for us from what we would consciously say we prefer. We may say that we want to be wealthy, but year after year we just barely make it. We may say that we want to be loved, but when a potential lover appears we shy away. We may say that we want to be fun-loving and popular, but we are restrained. What we say we want and the way we act may be contradictory. By looking around at what is, we know what (unconsciously) we have chosen.

Why would our subpersonalities prefer pain or deprivation rather than love and abundance? Because we act according to feelings and beliefs which are not conscious. We cling to "truths" about ourselves which our rational Adult minds did not choose, but which have been implanted by our Child minds in their attempt to understand reality. We think: Why would Dad hit me when he sees my toys on the floor? Because he loves me and wants me to learn responsibility. I'm so lazy he has to treat me that way. It's for my own good. He knows what's best for me. When I get hit, he's just telling me he loves me and wants the best for me. Or: Mom never has time for me, I guess I'm not an interesting person. Probably no one will want to stay around me very long. Or: Dad wasn't there for me when I needed protection. I guess I can't count on males to take care of me. Or: Mom says she loves me but she hates it when I cry. Crying must be a bad thing. I'll do what she likes and not cry.

By the time we're teenagers, our unconscious subpersonalities have constructed a world in which these Child beliefs are confirmed. Our familiar patterns of interacting are replicated. We have internalized the world we became used to as children, in the form of different subpersonalities (an Abusive Man, a Submissive Woman, an angry but withdrawn Child, or whatever else we experienced). That childhood world continues inside our heads. We have constructed an inner world based on experience, and this inner world gets projected around us for us to see.

We need to understand how we are responsible for creating our current realities before we can change. There is a whole complex world in our heads, constructed out of old beliefs. We need to move through that world to reach our goals. We can't tunnel under it or fly over it. It exists. Our beliefs form our realities. What we see around us just reflects what we (unconsciously) believe to be true. The form in which our beliefs are manifest can help us to discover what the beliefs are. The form itself isn't as important as what creates it: our unconscious beliefs. And these beliefs "live" through our subpersonalities.

Only dating ungiving men tells you that one of your subpersonalities is ungiving. Frequently meeting angry women tells you that you have an angry female subpersonality who is trying to be heard by you. When we can't hear from our subpersonalities directly, they will use another person's voice to get our attention. When we see patterns in our encounters, we know a subpersonality is manifesting, wanting to communicate with us.

So, when we feel blocked in reaching our goals—professional, financial or relational—we need to look to the inner world. Our subpersonalities are in conflict with each other. And the way we learned to handle conflicts as children will be recreated among our subpersonalities. The abusive Parental figure may dominate the scared Child for awhile but somehow it is always frustrated in its attempts to maintain the order it wants. The Child makes itself felt eventually! Perhaps that's what happened in your home when you were growing up—a controlling parent didn't listen to an unhappy child's voice, but there was always a point when that child broke through the control. A voice can be denied for only so long. And if denial was what you saw in interactions among people you knew when you were growing up, that's how your subpersonalities learned to resolve conflicts. "Listen to one voice and ignore any others. Do what you should, not what you want."

After many years of practicing a certain pattern of interacting—a Controlling Parent/Submissive Child, an Angry Critic/Rebellious Teenager, an Ascetic Monk/Frivolous Flirt, or whatever our primary subpersonality conflict is—we find ourselves stuck. Then we need to handle our inner conflicts differently. And the first step is to acknowledge what *is*. There tend to be two main subpersonalities involved (although we can learn to define and hear many voices) which reflect your basic polarity between what you accept and what you project.

Perhaps our inner Ambitious Entrepreneur wants to be a millionaire but the Deprived Child believes that having anything for herself is dangerous. Or the Lover may want to be married, but the Rejected Child believes that no one will stay with her for long. Or the Successful Professional can only function when the

Loser is out of sight. The frustration one subpersonality experiences in attempting to reach her goals spotlights the conflicting needs/beliefs of another subpersonality.

Often, the Controller's need to insure that our Child's rage doesn't explode and damage someone wins out over the Child's need to be spontaneous or to receive love. Altering the balance in whatever equilibrium exists between two subpersonalities means that the repressed voice will be heard more loudly. We may not be ready for this, so we maintain the status quo.

Whatever we choose (and we can see what we've chosen by looking around us), for some reason seems a wise choice. Often it appears to be safe. We may want spontaneity, freedom, appreciation, but feeling safe comes first before any of those things. So, somehow the subpersonalities have reached an acceptable equilibrium in what is.

If we don't like what we see around us, a natural inclination is to try to change what we see that we don't like. But, as we realize that our outer reality is a projection of an inner belief system, we will find it much faster and easier to change what is within us that is blocking us. For the outer world won't change until the inner world has changed. **It's no use trying to change a mirror if you don't like the reflection.**

However, some people are not at a point where they can recognize that they have any responsibility for their reality. Victims refuse to acknowledge this concurrence of the outer world with the inner. Victims prefer to accept no responsibility for creating their realities and give all the responsibility to others. They identify with one subpersonality and ignore, and therefore project, another subpersonality, seeing it only in someone else, not in themselves.

I always feel victimized by Victims. They place total responsibility for their feelings onto me without recognizing the strong, insistent pull they emit. They, unconsciously, need someone to mistreat them. They need me to be their Bad Guy so that they may continue their Victim denial.

Relating to Victims is frustrating. Either I am frustrated because I sense a certain pull from their unconscious, asking me to mistreat them, and I refuse but have to struggle with the tension within me. Or, if they are subtle and practiced at being a Victim, I get sucked into their game unawares and end up saying something which shocks me with its callousness. Then they believe that their view of the world as cruel and ungiving has been confirmed again.

In fact, those of us who come in contact with Victims are very responsive to them. They just won't see that we do exactly what they, unconsciously, ask us to do. They need to remain Victims to continue their denial and avoidance of responsibility for creating their own realities. If they truly took responsibility, they would have to consider how they are contributing to a reality in which they are always the Helpless Child. Someone else always has the power and effectiveness. They don't give their own internal Responsible Adult time or energy. They refuse to see the restrictive controlling Parent subpersonality inside of themselves, but they see it everywhere outside of themselves.

We all, to some extent, "get" people to react to us in response to our dominant subpersonality. It's unconscious on our part and on theirs. We end up in a dance to an unheard tune. We collude with them and they with us. Every Victim, therefore, needs to engage a Victimizer in his/her dance. How else can s/he play the Victim role?

If all the different subpersonalities were equally powerful, the Victim wouldn't be allowed to predominate. The other subpersonalities would limit her. Many of us indulge one subpersonality, giving it too much time and energy, allowing it to dominate, and grab center stage. Victims indulge the Helpless Child.

When she was young, Sharon's parents were emotionally cold, neglectful and abusive. She felt "rejected." Actually, she probably was rejected. Her parents probably didn't want a child and didn't want to hear her Child feelings and needs. Sharon left home after her emotionally tumultuous junior high and high school years and hasn't spoken with her parents for over twenty years.

Sharon is an attractive woman in her early forties, with round, dark eyes and curly ash blonde hair. She is short and slender and always well pressed. A characteristic mannerism for Sharon is clenching her fists and slightly squinting her eyes. She punctuates her sentences with this gesture for emphasis. She crosses her legs and an unseen motor moves her foot rhythmically in the air. Her small body seems tightly coiled, tension compressed in all her muscles.

On every special occasion—her birthday, Christmas, Mother's Day—Sharon is disappointed. She doesn't believe that her husband and two children love her enough or give her enough attention. Regardless of what her family does, she ends the day in tears, feeling rejected. This pattern has continued for years. Her children feel frustrated by their inability to convince her of their caring and her husband now refuses to continue to try to assuage her unloved feelings.

During an imagery session, Sharon requested that the part of her with strong feelings show herself. Sharon received an image of the Rejected Child as a fat, ten-year-old girl. She had two dark braids and was wearing plaid shorts. Either she walked in a small circle or sat in a corner with her head down. She obviously was miserable.

When she spoke, she sounded fearful and pathetic. She explained, "No one cares, no one ever has, no one could possibly love me. Something's wrong with me. I'm not like other people. I don't know why not. Something's missing in me. Even when people act like they love me, pretty soon they don't love me anymore. No one sticks around."

Sharon talked with this Child every few days over the next weeks. Whenever someone in Sharon's life seemed friendly, the Child would become excited, thinking, "This is it! This is the person who will understand me and love me and stay with me." Each time, the Child was disappointed. She became more and more depressed and convinced of her own unworthiness. Sharon truly appeared to be a pathetic figure when she was identified with her Rejected Child. Her shoulders drooped, she sighed and her voice became faint. I could understand why someone would want to try to rescue her from this misery.

I could also understand why that someone would leave her. She was completely identified with her miserable Rejected Child! When she was overwhelmed with the Child's need and hopelessness, no one else's voice could be heard. She couldn't even see that anyone else existed. She was as blind to real people outside of her as she was to all the other subpersonalities inside of her. The Rejected Child believed that no one could love her and didn't believe any contrary evidence. In the end, the Rejected Child was always proven right.

Her Rejected Child knew what it was like to experience rejection, expected it, and construed many interactions as being rejecting. It didn't matter what others intended. The Rejected Child was quick to spot the rejection she awaited. And she always found it, no matter how long it took, or how much reinterpretation of events she had to do. Her experience of being rejected always confirmed her belief that no one would love her. And maintaining that belief seemed ultimately important. Her husband believed Sharon was so attached to the Rejected Child and to maintaining that Child's reality, that she was unwilling to experience a more Adult, but less intense, shared reality with others. In a sense, Sharon was addicted to the intensity of the Rejected Child's feelings. But after years of disappointments in so many relationships, Sharon did want to realign her interactions. Finally exhausted, she was unwilling to continue the pattern of hope, disappointment, frustration and depression that the Child seemed to maintain. Sharon agreed with my suggestion that some other subpersonality could intervene to alter this self-destructive cycle.

The Rejected Child was so prominent with Sharon, receiving so much of her time and energy, that it was hard to hear from any other inner voice. Still, whenever Sharon was listening to her voices and she heard from the Rejected Child, she listened and thanked the Child for expressing herself verbally. As long as Sharon could hear the Child's words, she didn't have to act out the Child's drama, because allowing the unconscious to become conscious dilutes its energy. After the Child had finished speaking, Sharon was quiet and invited any other subpersonality to speak to her. Over several days another figure began to differentiate herself. An image of an older woman became clearer. "Severe" described her tightly pulled back hair, her fitted clothing and her drawn facial expression. Her air was self-righteous as she looked down her long pointed nose. She felt virtuous knowing that the Rejected Child was suffering. Her work seemed to be to continue the Child's pain.

This figure told the Rejected Child that other people were responsible for her suffering, and the Rejected Child resented these people. This new subpersonality did not take responsibility for her own part in the Child's dramas. She said, "I need the Rejected Child to suffer because as she suffers, I'm attacking her parents. They must be terrible parents if their daughter suffers so much. I'm punishing them by prolonging the Rejected Child's suffering."

When Sharon heard this statement, she named the new subpersonality the Angry Martyr. Did you ever, as a child, become angry with your parent, go to your room to cry, and then prolong the crying, even when you felt better, just to "get back at" your parent? This was the sentiment that motivated the Angry Martyr. She fueled the Child's suffering and wanted it to continue. She gave the Child messages which deflated her. The Child didn't evaluate the messages, she just swallowed them whole and felt the resultant feelings.

The Angry Martyr worked to keep the Child in pain. When the Child was hopeful or excited about a new relationship, the Angry Martyr was unseen. But shortly she reappeared with a huge bang, overwhelming the Child with an onrush of painful statements which the Child always took as truth. The Angry Martyr wouldn't let the Child receive love for very long. If the Child said, "I like my new friend; we're going to have lots of fun together," the Angry Martyr would say, "What makes you think she'll like you?" If the Child said, "I'm so happy today. I want to enjoy the rest of the week just like today," the Angry Martyr would say, "That will all change fast enough; it always does. Just remember the problem from last week. You need to be thinking about that." No matter what the Child would say the Angry Martyr had a deflating response.

After months of listening and observing her subpersonalities, Sharon had come to an understanding of her psychodynamics. She understood that the Angry Martyr needed the Child to suffer so she could continue to blame others and avoid responsibility. She realized that the Child thought being depressed was being good—doing just what an older subpersonality (the Angry Martyr) wanted. At least the Child was getting approval from someone, even if she had to hurt to do it. She wanted approval so much that she would do anything for it. Subtly, the Angry Martyr was rewarding the Child for being depressed. When the Child/Sharon was depressed, the Angry Martyr wouldn't criticize her or emphasize her unworthiness. There was some relief from the haranguing. But only as long as the depression lasted. When the Child began to feel better or to hope that her experience would be more joyful, then the Angry Martyr began with her messages again. She inflicted pain by repeatedly telling the Child that she was unlovable. These messages were so subtle that Sharon's Child had been hearing them for years without questioning them. It didn't even seem like a distinct voice; to the Child it was just the truth.

Thus, in her quest for love, the Child had a need to suffer—that was how she would receive the Angry Martyr's love. She was being good when she was depressed. Her life was predictable and no one could surprise her—she wasn't available to receive something that might be snatched away from her later.

As the Angry Martyr's malevolent intent became clearer, another subpersonality spontaneously arose. A masculine figure in his forties said, "I don't like what I see happening between the Angry Martyr and the Rejected Child. The Angry Martyr is abusing the Child, who doesn't know how to take care of herself. The Child can't put limits on the Martyr. The Child needs protection." Sharon named this new subpersonality the Reasonable Adult. He was outraged by the behavior of the Angry Martyr and wanted to intervene.

Sharon watched these three figures interact. She noticed how the Child took center stage, with the Angry Martyr always close but unseen in the shadows. When the Child felt hurt for an extended period of time, Sharon listened for the voice of the Angry Martyr. The Angry Martyr was subtle in her manipulation, but the pain indicated that she had been active.

After careful observation of the feelings of her inner figures, Sharon could discern the effects of the Angry Martyr. With continued attention, Sharon could even hear the Angry Martyr's voice as she spoke to the Child. "He doesn't really care about you. He'll think of someone else as soon as he's gone. You can't trust him. You're going to be alone again. No one will ever really want to be close to you." Sharon recognized the Child's fears as being her experience *after* listening to the Angry Martyr. The

Child totally believed the Angry Martyr and was not sophisticated enough to confront the Angry Martyr.

When Sharon could identify clearly what her Rejected Child felt and what her Angry Martyr said, she could call on her Reasonable Adult. He wanted the Child to be free of the Angry Martyr's oppressive statements. To the Angry Martyr he stated, "Your words are not truth. You hate and hurt. You don't want joy and happiness. You are committed to suffering and separation between the Child and anyone else." The Reasonable Adult could see that the Angry Martyr was trying to protect the Rejected Child from even greater hurt by keeping her continually in a lesser amount of pain. This "lesser" pain kept the Child afraid of closeness, so she would never risk the greater pain that can come from loving and losing. Still, the Reasonable Adult wasn't willing to agree to that bargain. By clearly describing the dynamics between the Child and the Martyr, he provided the Rejected Child with protection against abuse from the Angry Martyr. He constructed a shield for the Child against the Martyr's words by interpreting the Martyr's intent to the Child. In this way, the person of the Martyr was seen and evaluated. The Reasonable Adult had to do this for the Child; she was incapable of such critical thinking herself.

No longer did the Child need to view the subtle destructive messages as truth. Now she could understand that these hateful statements came from an angry subpersonality who wanted to hurt her. The Angry Martyr became a figure of whom to be wary. She would damage if she could. With the insights the Reasonable Adult had given to Sharon, Sharon could now see and hear the Angry Martyr distinctly. Therefore, her words could be questioned and her motives clarified.

But then the Child's voice became audible. She said, "I want someone to love me." Sharon knew there must be an inner subpersonality who could love the Child. Through her experience in relationships and with her new knowledge of the dynamics of her subpersonalities, she knew that her Child's needs for love would first have to be met by an inner figure before they could be met by a real person.

Sharon asked to be shown an image of that inner figure. She closed her eyes, breathed and waited. Watching her spontaneous imagery, Sharon described a Nurturing Mother. "She is dressed in a long, full-skirted calico dress. She resembles a pioneer woman. She looks like she could have established a home in the wilderness."

I suggested to Sharon that she invite the Nurturing Pioneer Mother to establish a home inside of Sharon for her Child. Sharon did so and watched. She saw the Nurturing Pioneer Mother clean a small cabin, bringing in flowers and fixing a meal of fresh vegetables. The Mother arranged a corner where she could hold the Child and tell her stories.

Sharon was surprised by the industriousness of this figure as she prepared a space in which to nurture the Child. The Nurturing Pioneer Mother readied herself to welcome the Child by spending a few minutes alone and then looking up and calling to the Child. The Child came slowly from around a corner. The Nurturing Pioneer Mother invited her to sit on her large lap. The Child crawled up hesitantly and waited to see what would happen to her. The Nurturing Pioneer Mother sang softly and rocked the Child. After several minutes, the Child's body relaxed and she rested her head on the Mother's breast. The Mother continued to sing and hum and the Child dozed. Even while the Child slept, the Mother held her and sang so that when the Child awoke she was still being rocked.

With variations, this scene occurred weekly. The Child became accustomed to the constancy of the Mother's reassuring presence. She grew into a "body understanding" of what receiving care and attention felt like. Usually, the Child would sleep and her body would soak up the caring from the Pioneer Mother's enfolding larger body. The transfer of love was unconscious between the Mother and the Child as Sharon watched.

Sharon saw the Child grow taller and slimmer, feeling confident and strong. The Child incorporated the Mother's concern for her and she grew up having concern for herself. Her body knew she had a home even when she didn't focus her thoughts upon that fact.

As Sharon watched these scenes of the Nurturing Pioneer Mother and the Child, her own real life adult experience shifted. She wrote in her journal at this time:

> Within myself I am comfortable and with others I am happy. My inner Child has received the caring she so desperately wanted and now other people seem supportive and loving to me! When I saw the reactions of my husband and children change, I had to realize that in the past I had been instrumental, unconsciously, in affecting how they treated me. Now that I'm listening more to the Nurturing Pioneer Mother within me, I receive more nurturing from around me.
>
> Now that I experience my life working the way I want it to, I realize that I haven't been depressed and oppressed all of these years because my real parents rejected me. All I was doing by blaming my parents was refusing to take responsibility for my own life, for how that inner Angry Martyr was oppressing and rejecting my inner Child. I was allowing that Child to be victimized by that Martyr and then was blaming my parents for my pain! When I saw how dramatically my experience shifted after the internal work I did, without my parents' involvement, I fully understood that my parents were not responsible for my pain, but that my Angry Martyr was.

There was a time in Sharon's childhood when she wasn't responsible for the experience in her life. Children cannot be blamed for any miserable situations in which they live. But the role Sharon had learned during childhood was continued during adulthood without regard to her situation in reality. **Just as children cannot be blamed for their own suffering, adults cannot blame their own suffering on anyone else.**

Sharon's process shows how she needed to re-create the rejection and pain of her childhood. She wasn't ready to leave that behind and change the beliefs her Angry Martyr had fed her Child all of her life. She needed to hold onto those beliefs, act them out in relationships, experience her loneliness, and finally realize how she was responsible for maintaining that pain.

When Sharon noticed how identifying with the Rejected Child had led her to be unaware of the Angry Martyr, she began to reconsider how she had made sense of her experience in the world. If she had failed to notice the Angry Martyr who was so influential inside of her, what else had she not noticed? Had she chosen to ignore certain things in the outside world?

Sharon began to wonder if her mother were really as cold and unresponsive as she had perceived her to be. She realized that she hadn't known her mother as a person in her own right, that she had only known her as the powerful person who disappointed Sharon as a child. Now that Sharon was no longer identified with being a Rejected Child, her view of her mother widened. She was willing to see her as a human being with a life of her own, with a past, with feelings, and with her own disappointments. She even started to wonder what their twenty-year separation had been like for her mother.

Soon her curiosity led her to write to her mother. She had sworn that she would never again have contact with "that woman" but now she wondered who "that woman" was.

She wrote shyly at first. She told her mother about her life now. She didn't mention therapy or the past. She let her mother know some details about her everyday world with her family and her job. She kept her letter short and invited her mother to write back. Sharon received her mother's reply within a week. Her mother expressed intense sorrow over their long separation and described what her life had been like at the time of their last contact.

Over several months during which they exchanged letters frequently, Sharon grew to appreciate that her mother had been unhappy with her own life when Sharon was a child and unable to respond to her daughter's misery. Sharon was surprised to learn that her mother had known, and had cared very deeply, that Sharon had been unhappy. Her mother just hadn't felt powerful enough to do anything about it.

In her journal, Sharon considered the notion that her mother wasn't all-powerful:

> I've always thought of my mother as a towering giant. I thought she could do everything! I'm sure I first saw her that way when I was very small and her bigness was such a contrast. I was so afraid of her and wanted so badly for her to love me that I thought if she didn't, it was my fault. Someone who looked so big and so powerful to me couldn't be mistaken! I was sure that if only I could be different, she would love me. I felt totally powerless and saw her as totally powerful. I thought she could protect me from everything I feared. (I sure wanted her to!) Now I can understand that she couldn't even protect herself. She must have been overwhelmed with the care of a baby at seventeen. When I was seventeen, I wasn't even thinking clearly. I can't imagine starting a family at that age!
>
> She probably was a good woman but she must have been frightened herself. No wonder she couldn't protect me from my fears; she couldn't even handle her own. My feelings must have reminded her of her own painful feelings. I was a threat to her! Isn't it funny how all my life I've thought only of what I've wanted from her, not of what she wanted. I must have made her life impossible! Even at twenty-five, when I conceived my first child, and I wanted him very much, I still resented the pressure sometimes. Every mother must. My mother didn't know that her resentment was natural. She just tried to get by the best way she could. I needed her so desperately when I was young. And I was so terribly disappointed. That never convinced me to stop trying to receive what I wanted her to give me. I chose depression over releasing my hopes that I would receive love in the way I wanted from her.

> Now I can honestly release those wants. She doesn't have to be my protector anymore. I don't need her to be all-powerful and all-knowing. I have my own protection and support from inside me. That is really where I need it, too.
>
> She did her very best. Would I have done that well at seventeen? She looks so different to me now. If I had just met her and didn't need her or depend on her, I would think she was well-intentioned but in a lot of pain herself. She didn't know how to relate to her own inner Child so, of course, she couldn't respond to me as a child. No one had ever taken care of her, so she didn't know how to take care of me.
>
> Her Frightened Child was the biggest part of her when I was a child. I thought she was tyrannical and uncaring. But she wasn't only my parent. She was living her own life and that was very, very painful for her. She chose a facade of Someone Without Feelings in order to survive those hard years. Now I know that she was just dealing with her own Frightened Child in the only way she knew how. When I see her Frightened Child and identify with my Nurturing Parent I don't feel angry with her. I feel powerful in my own life and in my own body. I can take care of myself from within me!
>
> I realize now that we're all in this life together. No one gets a head start. We can walk with each other or push everyone away but we're all walking the same path. It's more important to learn how to walk the path than to resent the other walkers. Walking with integrity and responsibility is the real challenge.

Sharon realized that she had maintained her own depression as a way of assuming responsibility for her mother's lack of responsiveness to her. In that way the Child part of her could avoid being angry with her mother, and she could maintain her image of her mother as all-powerful and all-good.

As long as the Angry Martyr had been prominent, Sharon had felt the need to avoid her mother. As she resolved her internal conflicts with the Angry Martyr her relationship with her mother shifted.

The Angry Martyr, a part of Sharon she didn't know and didn't take responsibility for, had been projected onto her mother. When Sharon heard the Angry Martyr clearly and directly within her, she didn't need to project that energy. She owned it and worked with it internally by having the Reasonable Adult relate to the Martyr and the Child.

As her inner clarity increased, her outer relationships simplified. Now she could see her mother separately from her own needs and projections. As she withdrew her projections, her mother became a less powerful figure for Sharon.

From her identification with the Reasonable Adult, Sharon could relate to her mother and her own family with less inappropriate intensity. She was also open to receiving just what they had to offer her. She didn't need them to fit her fantasy. Sharon was satisfied with the lessened intensity. It didn't feel like she was losing aliveness, but gaining clarity and becoming grounded. She no longer needed anyone to rescue her or to change her daily experience. She could trust her feelings to take care of her, so she stopped demanding an uncommon amount of attention from other people. Consequently, her relationships were based on mutual enjoyment, not on an attempt to remedy a deficiency. Life could happen each day for that day, not as a response to past unresolved pain.

❦ ❦ ❦ ❦ ❦

We interact with others in the same way that our subpersonalities are interacting among themselves. We project one of our subpersonalities onto someone in our lives, and then totally identify with another subpersonality. Many of us believe that we shouldn't be powerful personally; that is, that we shouldn't accept our own needs and wants and guidance. We believe it is better to keep others comfortable and to maintain silence. Since we are not comfortable owning our own power, we may project it onto others. When we project power onto husbands, wives, friends, we remove them from the realm of being peers and structure a Parent-Child relationship. **It seems as though we need to continually create unequal power situations in which we can experience our feelings about being powerless until we can change them into experiences in which we are powerful.** This process takes many repetitions.

We must gradually become aware that we can have some control over how we are treated. We can't just let go of an image of ourselves as deprived and mistreated and, overnight, assume the posture of an effective, respectable soul. There is no going directly from the Frog to the Prince. The steps are small and the transformation gradual, but it does occur.

❦ ❦ ❦ ❦ ❦

Alice's husband seemed very powerful to her. Most adults seemed very powerful to Alice. She felt small, insignificant and unworthy of notice. These were feelings Alice had maintained since childhood. Her mother had exercised overwhelming control over her three daughters and her husband. When her mother wanted to go somewhere, everyone went. When she wanted to stay, no one's alternative suggestion was allowed. Her mother's wishes always prevailed.

Alice had learned from her father that the way to have power was to be invisible and passive-aggressive. He had learned to live with a dominating woman without losing his own individuality. He didn't express himself directly but learned to resist her subtly, by indirectly frustrating her. When his wife wanted to go, he would get ready, but usually couldn't find something he needed, so the family would wait. When she chose to stay, he was restless, often grumbling or irritable. Without saying much, he made his presence uncomfortably felt.

By watching her father, Alice learned how to annoy others without taking responsibility for her actions. She had internalized an image of a powerless figure who made people uncomfortable while proclaiming his own powerlessness ("Who, me?").

Alice's personal power scared her. She feared the consequences of stating her feelings and her wants clearly. Since she wanted very much to be taken care of, she wouldn't risk exposing any part of herself she thought others would dislike. She needed to maintain connections to potential caregivers regardless of the cost. And the cost was her integrity.

She felt natural impulses to assert who she was but believed this would lead to abandonment. Being "known" was dangerous. Therefore, her own wants and preferences took on an ominous quality. If she expressed herself honestly and directly, she didn't know what reaction she might receive. She also didn't know the limits of her own aggression (What will I do? How far will I go if I don't restrain myself? What irreparable damage will I do? What will my family do if they truly see who I am?).

A subpersonality developed who housed those parts of Alice she feared would lead her to ultimate aloneness. She called it the Little Devil. This Devil contained her strong feelings, assertiveness and wants. Like Alice's father, the Devil was concerned with resisting the control of others. This resistance was the only way Alice knew of to be "powerful."

Her husband said that Alice was very effective in gaining what she wanted. She nagged, cried and complained. And she always felt resentful. She felt herself to be a Victim and she didn't understand how she could be otherwise. She wanted someone to take care of her, to understand her needs and wants without her having to verbalize them.

Alice's appearance betrayed the quality of care she took of herself. She was generally disordered, her wrinkled shirts and skirts almost, but not quite, matching. Her hair was seldom arranged neatly and often was not clean. She gave the impression that she had barely been able to keep our appointment. She seemed to have emerged from chaos with adequate respectability to appear in the office but not with a strong sense that she was set to continue her day. There was always a sense of something left unfinished; I guessed that she didn't usually make her bed. Her hazel eyes seldom met mine. She examined her nails, the furniture, the ceiling. She seemed not to want to relate to me too directly. I wondered if she really knew what I looked like.

Alice believed that her role in life was to make others comfortable by anticipating their needs and providing what they wanted (this was how she wanted others to treat her, too). She nurtured and cared for her family and responded to them. She didn't consciously listen to her own wants or live her own life from any inner direction. She was consciously focused on others, gaining direction for her actions from them. She acted the part of the Selfless Caretaker. (Her Devil was hidden, unconscious, but still very much present.)

When her three children left home, Alice was lost. Her husband, Hank, had tired of her whining and spent little time with her. Her passive-aggressive manipulations were futile; there was no one around who would react to her. Now she could no longer center her life on others' behavior. She recognized that her own life wasn't working and that *she* would have to be the one to change.

In therapy we wanted to develop those parts of Alice which had not previously been developed. Since she had emphasized the feminine trait of nurturing through so much of her life, we looked for a masculine voice inside of her which would provide balance. For several weeks she was quiet in her meditations, watching for signs of a masculine presence.

Eventually, she met a subpersonality she called John. John was a kind of vehicle for the Devil because through his passivity, anger (a Devil characteristic) was expressed. John was a middle-aged man who was submissive, gentle, sweet. A pleasant but ineffectual figure, John's facade was similar to that of Alice's father. Alice liked him immediately and found talking with him to be supportive. John seemed to know all the right things to say to Alice to make her feel valued. However, she felt his lack of power. She didn't know if she could trust him to protect her in a crisis. She guessed that he wouldn't be there for her.

After more weeks in which Alice listened quitely, another masculine voice differentiated itself. Greg was rough, uncouth, aggressive—unlike anyone Alice knew. Greg could angrily make himself felt. He was a more active, direct vehicle for the Devil than John. Alice recoiled from confronting his anger directly. She didn't like or trust Greg. She found him "offensive." She ignored him and didn't listen to his voice unless I suggested it.

One day, she was mugged by a man who stole her purse. Alice was terribly upset. In our session the next afternoon, she asked Greg if he knew anything about the incident. He replied, "Yes, I knew what was happening. I saw the entire scene. And I wanted it to happen to you. You ignore me, but a man finally got to you. Maybe now you've learned your lesson."

Greg had wanted her attention and had chosen this dramatic way to get it. When Alice heard him say that he knew what had happened to her, including the pain which she had experienced, she realized that those parts of her which she refused to recognize and which, thereby, were shoved into her unconscious, still powerfully affected her.

If Greg had known what had happened to her, he probably was also involved in creating it, Alice surmised. When she asked him if he were, he said, "Yes," but offered no explanation. On a physical level, part of Alice's unconscious (Greg) had worked effectively to sabotage her. This was a sobering and frightening revelation for Alice. She was angry with Greg for his part in the mugging and now felt like his victim. But she also realized that she needed to take him seriously. Ignoring him was costly emotionally and dangerous physically. She had preferred to pretend that he didn't exist but could no longer afford that easy escape.

Alice spent time listening to Greg over the next weeks. She was not anxious to know him; she was just terrified of what might happen to her if she didn't. When she paid attention to him, he responded to her honestly and directly. Usually Alice consulted him about business concerns (she didn't trust him enough yet to talk to him about her feelings). Greg advised her to negotiate in a forthright manner and to be assertive about what she wanted.

Because she was listening to him, he no longer tried to hurt her surreptitiously. Greg encouraged Alice to identify with him and let him do the talking when she needed to make a business deal. He didn't care if anyone else liked him, he just wanted to be effective in getting what he thought he deserved. During this time, Alice had to negotiate a new contract at work. Previously, her Victim would have entered the meeting unprepared and left feeling resentful. Greg asked to be in charge and Alice agreed. He planned his short speech, outlined his requirements, and presented himself professionally. Everything that Alice/Greg requested was included in her contract.

Alice used Greg successfully in several negotiations at work and at home and was pleased. There was no emotional wrangling and no guilt. In fact, emotions didn't come into the picture at all.

Alice, however, was still angry with Greg for "participating" in the mugging. She told him so (having learned assertion from him) and then asked for an apology. Greg replied, "The mugging was something you forced to happen. You didn't listen to me and didn't even want to know I existed. The Selfless Caretaker was the only person you listened to. Well, it's too bad it had to happen, but you could have treated me differently."

When we push parts of ourselves out of our awareness and continue to ignore them, they gain intensity and power. They continue to operate, but without our awareness. Consequently, we don't know what they are doing. They still exist and, because we no longer monitor their actions, they may behave destructively and we are blind to it. We have wanted to keep them in the dark, but we are really in the dark because we have chosen to be ignorant of that part of ourselves. That, essentially, allows the unwanted subpersonality total freedom without our awareness which can be very dangerous. It is likely we will feel the result with intense pain. We can't ignore any part of ourselves and escape untouched. What we have chosen to keep unconscious gets acted out towards, or within, the body. Choosing not to listen to the unconscious can have serious physical consequences.

Alice felt forced to relate to Greg in self-defense; she didn't want his anger directed at her again. Although she didn't want to admit that any part of her had the characteristics she ascribed to Greg, she had to acknowledge that there was an irrefutable correlation between her denial of him and her feeling of being victimized by other people. This became clear to her through her journal writing. It wasn't anyone in particular she could accuse of trying to hurt her; she was just the Loser in general. After acknowledging her subpersonalities and observing their dynamics between each other and in relationship to other people, Alice understood that she was making her life turn out as it was. Unconsciously, she had been clinging to her Victim/Loser identification and repressing Greg. Now, after so much pain, Alice thought that she was ready to relinquish the Loser subpersonality. In her journal, her Adult wrote:

> I don't know how it has happened, but losing has become my way of being in relationship to the world. I have the feeling that everyone wants to take something from me. I never think that anyone would want to talk to me or be interested in my opinions.

At that moment Greg intruded:

Greg: You don't want to know *my* opinions. You only talk to me to insure your safety.

Adult: Are you saying that I treat you the way other people treat me?

Greg: I'm saying that you need to acknowledge how you mistreat me. You ignore me and stifle my voice and then you whine when you feel treated that way by others. Well, I say hooray! You're only getting what you deserve. You think you can just decide that I don't exist and "poof," I'll disappear. Well, damn it, you're going to acknowledge me somehow!

Adult: Whoa. You are very upset.

Greg: Damn right! So are you when you feel ignored. You should understand exactly how I feel!

Adult: I'm blocking you out and you're reacting the same way I do. I never realized what I was doing!

Greg: You've been so self-righteous! You make me sick with all your complaining about how much you give and how little support you receive and then you turn around and suffocate me. Well, I won't let you kill me, you bitch. I'm going to live as long as you do, and longer maybe, and every time you hurt me, you're going to get it right back! Don't think you're stronger than I am. You may win small victories, but I'll never let you be at peace as long as you judge me "offensive." Well, perhaps I am offensive, but what I'm offended at is your high and mighty attitude that you're so good and I'm so awful. Bullshit!! I'll show you awful!

Adult: OK, OK. I had no idea you were so upset. The way you explain it, your feelings are perfectly understandable. It's healthy, in fact, that you don't want to die. And I've been trying to kill you! We've been conducting intense warfare and I didn't even know it! Let's not do this any longer. We can find another way to relate. We don't need to fight continually.

Greg: I only fight because you force me to. I will not be killed!

Adult: I will not try to kill you, I promise. I will offer you what I want—acceptance. I will listen to you and not judge you.

> Greg didn't respond. My Adult sensed that he was no longer furious. I've opened a door for him. He no longer needs to bang on it.

Over the next months, Alice's Adult listened to Greg. Sometimes he ranted irrationally, sometimes he criticized her, and sometimes he just told her what he wanted. No matter what he said, Alice's Adult listened and accepted it.

As the Adult's attitude toward Greg shifted, his manner changed also. Gradually, he became softer. He spoke more slowly and swore less. He seemed to feel more relaxed as the threat of annihilation by the Adult was removed.

Greg and John had each dialogued with the Adult. Now they talked with each other. Alice spent many hours observing their interactions, watching as they became acquainted. As they began to know each other better, they started to appreciate each other and learn when their own personal style was appropriate to the situation and when they should call in the other one. They cooperated in reaching common goals. Eventually they didn't dialogue formally as separate individuals, but quickly and subtly communicated.

In the next weeks, as Greg's "softening" continued, Alice could no longer distinguish him from John. Initially, they had such different personalities. But as Greg's hostility diminished so did John's passivity. They seemed to be moving from opposite ends of a continuum toward a center point. This was not something

Alice had thought about and chosen. She just watched this merging happen. This new masculine figure had the beneficial qualities of both John and Greg without either one's "weakness." She noticed Greg's assertiveness without his bulldozing aggression and John's gentleness without his passive-aggressive compliance.

Alice finally grew to trust her new masculine figure. She had spent hours listening to him and had watched his evolution from two extreme figures into one strong, centered male. John and Greg had grown together. Alice liked their fusion and appreciated her Inner Male. Because she had invested so much of her time and energy in the relationship with him, she knew him well and trusted him. She committed herself to always being available to him.

She knew that he welcomed her commitment because her interactions with others became gratifying. No longer did she need to approach others in a roundabout manner. Manipulation and passive-aggression were not her standard means of interacting any longer. She no longer identified with the Loser; in fact, she couldn't even find that subpersonality inside of her. Without conscious effort she protected and supported herself in relationships. She owned her own power. Therefore, she had no need to project it onto others and struggle with them. She had taken responsibility for the discord in her relationships. By listening and responding, she had allowed Greg and John to grow. Their needs were met and their voices respected. When she supported them, they worked for her. As she acknowledged their voices, they became an integral and integrated part of her.

Alice wrote in her journal:

> I suppose the changes have been slow in coming. Over these last two years, my marriage has become totally different from how it was for ten years. Hank has begun courting me again! I had forgotten the little bouquets of wild flowers he used to bring me, but now they have reappeared. There are other nice small touches

that remind me of our affection for each other. When we were polarized into our roles—my Child/his Parent, my Victim/his Victimizer—we didn't trust each other. We didn't share vulnerability. We wouldn't get too close to each other but we couldn't let go, either. We just maintained a resentful stalemate.

Sometimes there were angry eruptions after which we didn't speak for two or three days, but mostly we believed (I can see now) that the other was the adversary, someone to be scrutinized and to be wary of. We never could fully relax around each other. Yet, when we tried parting, we feared losing the other's protection. I hated Hank for his lack of response to me, but the thought of not having his stabilizing influence in my life terrified me. I needed him, but feared him, and that usually showed in my little ways of pressuring him and putting him down.

As I feel more competent, stronger and better able to take care of myself, I feel more confidence than ever. When we married I had hoped he would protect me. When he didn't, I turned on him. Now that I can protect myself, I don't see him as evil. He isn't my enemy. When I first met him, I thought he would be my savior. Gradually, I realized he was human and couldn't save me from hurt. Then I felt cheated and I resented him. I thought he was just withholding the caretaking I wanted and "knew" he could give me. When I was mean to him, I was punishing him for not being what I wanted—someone who would save me from my own hurts.

He couldn't do that, but now I look for my own protection from inside me and not from Hank. John and Greg were the ones making my life hard, not Hank. Or, rather, John and Greg were just trying to survive and to be acknowledged by me. They needed my attention, not Hank.

It's hard work, looking at what is happening inside me. Being a Victim is easy. It's taking responsibility for my feelings and growing up that's hard. But that's the only way Hank and I can share true friendship—as equal, healthy partners.

Because Alice had worked to create and maintain an inner peace, her outer relationships were also peaceful. There was no internal warfare to be reflected to her in external realities, only cooperation and caring. When she maintained peace within her, she experienced it around her.

❧ ❧ ❧ ❧ ❧

Do you identify with Sharon or Alice? How?

_____
_____
_____
_____
_____
_____
_____
_____
_____

Describe your own Victim subpersonality (include gender, appearance, age, behavior):

_____
_____
_____
_____
_____
_____
_____
_____
_____
_____
_____
_____

When are you identified with your Victim subpersonality?

What is the characteristic statement you make to yourself or to others when your Victim dominates?

When does it "work" to be a Victim? What is the "payoff?"

What's going on inside you when you choose to act out the Victim subpersonality?

_____
_____
_____
_____
_____

Which other subpersonality in you could achieve what the Victim achieves but in a more direct, responsible way?

_____
_____
_____
_____

Relaxation

Spend several minutes doing the relaxation exercise on page 9.

Exercise

See yourself walking on a city street. Notice what is on your left and your right. (*Pause.*) There are people walking past you. Look at their faces. (*Pause.*) Some of the people walking towards you represent your subpersonalities. One of them will come up to you. Wait. (*Pause.*) When a figure approaches you notice the body posture, facial expression and breathing of the figure. (*Pause.*) Before that figure speaks, what message is s/he conveying to you non-verbally? (*Pause.*) Listen as that figure speaks to you. S/he will tell you something about him/herself. (*Pause.*) What "part of you" is s/he? (*Pause.*) What is his/her message to you? (*Pause.*) Thank him/her and walk on.

(*Pause.*) Does another figure approach you? Wait and watch. (*Pause.*) Notice who comes and what s/he says to you. (*Pause.*) Again, thank him/her and let him/her pass. If all the figures so far have been of one gender, see if there is anyone of the opposite gender who wants to approach you. (*Pause.*) Walk for as long as you would like and notice if any other figure approaches you. (*Pause.*) When you have walked so far that there are no other people around you, experience yourself treasuring the messages from these figures. (*Pause.*) Keep the messages with you and notice how you breathe and how you walk. (*Pause.*)

Describe each figure you met and the message from each figure:

_____
_____
_____
_____
_____
_____
_____
_____
_____
_____
_____
_____

What happened inside your body as you heard each message?

_____
_____
_____
_____
_____
_____

How does your body manifest your beliefs and conflicts?

Do you have any chronic illnesses?

Do you get cravings? What kind?

Where are you tense?

What could you be holding onto? What inner feelings are you avoiding?

Who is your seldom-heard-from inner masculine figure?

Who is your seldom-heard-from inner feminine figure?

Of all the figures you met during your walk whom do you like?

Whom do you dislike?

_____
_____
_____
_____
_____

Which of the subpersonalities you mentioned wants your attention? Take a few minutes, listen to that subpersonality, and record what you hear:

_____
_____
_____
_____
_____
_____
_____
_____
_____
_____
_____
_____
_____
_____
_____
_____
_____
_____
_____

Developing A Caring Parent 4

Jane is a beautiful woman, always impeccably dressed. Her subtle make-up emphasizes her large, blue eyes. Her purse, shoes and nails match whatever outfit she wears. She is tall and slender, resembling a model in the care she obviously takes with her appearance. In contrast to her "together" appearance, she seems uncomfortable on her first visits to me, swinging her foot, speaking quickly and seldom making eye contact. She later admits to having been embarrassed about needing a therapist.

The issue that brings Jane into therapy is her intense pain and frustration over not conceiving a child. She has been to all kinds of doctors; had two minor surgeries; dragged her husband, Mike, to examinations; tried artificial insemination and donor sperm. She kept charts and calendars and took her temperature daily. She did everything she was instructed to do, but getting pregnant was not something she could force by her own determination. If it were a matter of following directions, Jane would have accomplished her goal. But becoming pregnant was not a problem she could solve by taking action.

Mike is a recovering alcoholic; he hasn't had a drink for eight years. Jane is highly responsible and has supported the two of them for most of their thirteen-year marriage. Regularly there are crises, usually financial, usually precipitated by Mike. One day, while in a hurry, Mike forgets to set the parking brake in his car. The car rolls into the neighbor's new Cadillac and they have a bill for damages. Or, he might be distracted by a beautiful view and forget to watch his step. He falls twisting his ankle and is on crutches for six weeks. Each time Jane rescues Mike.

She tells me that she stays very busy: "There are bills to be paid; I have to concentrate on making money." And "I've made commitments; I can't disappoint people who depend on me." At other times she says, "I do everything right." She is angry and frustrated that doing everything right hasn't led to happiness or peace for her. She has learned all the rules and she follows them exactly. She tries hard.

I agree with her, saying, "It's not fair. You do everything right. Others probably don't perform as carefully as you do." We acknowledge that her way of being good isn't bringing her peace and conclude that "doing" must be irrelevant to personal satisfaction. Otherwise, she would have everything she wants. I explain to her that doing isn't the path and peace isn't a goal to be achieved—it's a process. When I ask Jane to take twenty minutes to sit and do nothing, she becomes noticeably agitated. Adamantly, she states that she cannot "do nothing." Doing nothing for her is watching television or working a crossword puzzle. I ask her to describe her fantasy of what would happen were she to do nothing. After a pause, she describes an image of a building falling apart around her, leaving her stuck in rubble with dust filling the air. When I ask her how she is freed from the "stuckness" in her image, she replies that since she can do nothing, she remains stuck. Remaining stuck, she dies.

Being active and busy insures Jane's survival in her own mind. She has always been effective in saving herself and Mike. When she can overcome adversity, she benefits. She feels reinforced as the One Who Shoulders the World's Burdens. As long as she has a project to work on, she can contain her anxiety and fear, shoving them aside for the moment. That way she can "manage" her feelings. She doesn't feel them very intensely and they don't interfere with her accomplishments. As long as she can prove to herself that she can solve any problem, she feels comforted. Temporarily.

Jane needs to continually prove to herself that she will survive because basically she fears that she won't. As a child she didn't learn to trust that someone capable would always be available to protect her. In fact, she learned that the comings and goings of those around her were unpredictable. She wasn't told, at the age of three, that her father was deploying with his Navy division for a year. She gradually and fearfully discovered that her protector was absent. "OK," she must have said to herself as a child, "If no one will protect me, I'll protect myself. I'll stay away from painful feelings. I'll act as if they don't exist."

She learned to avoid her pain with work. She believed that she couldn't "do" anything about her fear of loss, her anxiety about survival or her uncertainty about being loved. She also thought that she couldn't tolerate the pain of those feelings. But she could work hard. She focused her attention on work to hide her fears and doubts, avoiding vulnerability.

Before she married Mike, Jane believed that no one could love her and that she might be alone forever. This thought terrified her. So, of course, she jumped at the chance to be married. Maybe Mike drank excessively and abused drugs, but at least she could be Mrs. Somebody Else. That seemed to still some of the demons who tormented her with accusations of her unworthiness. Temporarily.

The first five years of their marriage were a "nightmare." She described Mike as being "out of control." He was arrested for drunk driving, received speeding tickets and might or might not come home each night. So, because her unconscious had already decided what to do in difficult situations, Jane focused her attention on working and on saving Mike from the predicaments he created. She rescued him repeatedly.

When Mike would create crises, Jane would muster her strength. When he was consumed with the volatility of his life, she would be steady. She received no emotional support from Mike and very little help financially.

After five years of marriage, Mike quit drinking and went to Alcoholics Anonymous. A few months later, Jane started attending Al-Anon meetings. She relinquished her more obvious rescues and their life together became somewhat more stable.

The fact that Mike didn't support her was, in a convoluted sense, comfortable for Jane. It reinforced her belief that "you can't count on anyone," and that it was better to deny her needs. Since her situation didn't allow her to be needy, she just would not acknowledge her needs. She had learned to deny them in childhood and continued her denial with Mike. Unconsciously, Jane was giving Mike a message to continue his outrageous acting-out behavior. She profited from it because with so much excitement outside of her, she couldn't afford to look inside and to feel the pain there. Mike offered her a compelling distraction from her inner world.

Without trying, Jane had developed a marriage relationship which mirrored the relationship between her prominent subpersonalities. Jane identified with Control while she denied and projected her vulnerable Child feelings and needs onto Mike.

Mike represented a part of Jane that she didn't want to see. Inside of her was pain and fear, while outside she maintained an appearance of total control. She didn't look into her inner world. She feared her feelings would overwhelm her Control and she might not survive. Jane had learned that survival depended upon Control. By refusing to acknowledge her vulnerable parts—her pain, her fear, her need—she created a reality in which they would be shown to her. She couldn't avoid it. She had to see outside of her in Mike what she didn't want to see inside of her.

Couples are together because they have something to learn from each other. One reflects the other's hidden, unconscious parts. If there is some quality that irks you and you don't want to see it in yourself, you'll be shown it in your mate or someone else in your life. We all seem to be here to help each other become clearer in our consciousness.

Who gets to you? Who can you really not stand? What qualities does that person manifest that you're refusing to see in yourself? What is the value of having that person in your life? (Yes, there is value. You need to see him/her, to know him/her so as to know yourself. If you don't want to know someone else, what is it *in you* that you don't want to know?)

There's no sense blaming your mate. You drew him/her into your life. So when you're annoyed with him/her, look inside of yourself for some unacceptable subpersonality who hasn't been heard. As long as Jane focused her attention on Mike and not on her hurt Child, she could not heal, and therefore nothing in her life could change significantly. You have a basic responsibility to heal your inner world. When you acknowledge this fact, you learn clearly and strongly the Universal Law of Non-Interference: **If it's not your life, don't try to live it.** You won't have time to manage someone else's affairs if you truly take responsibility for your own. If you do have time and energy to choreograph another's every movement, you are probably not giving your inner world all the attention it deserves.

As we attend to our needs and wounds internally, we notice consistencies with our outer world experience. We notice that the husband we have chosen elicits in us the same reactions we had earlier in life with a parent. Dependency with him works out the same way that dependency with a parent did. If we didn't receive much understanding from a parent, we probably won't receive much from a mate. If our needs were treated carefully in childhood, we learned to respect our needs; therefore, we project that care and draw to us someone who treats our needs carefully. We identify with our parents and unconsciously form our own internal Parent. Then we project that Parent onto a mate. But the essential middle step is the internal subpersonality we have each developed and for which we are responsible.

Conceiving a child was the only goal in Jane's life with which Control could not aid her. Thus, it was in this arena that she had to look into the parts of herself which she hadn't developed, her Shadow. This would be a major realization for Jane, acknowledging she would have to look to her feelings for her satisfaction. She was familiar with denying them, regarding them as troublesome and a source of irritation. For her to make this 180 degree shift indicated an acknowledgement of the existence of part of her she had never wanted to know. It was only because she could no longer avoid the overwhelming intensity of the pain coming from her inner world that she was even willing to consider this last resort.

With therapy, Jane became increasingly aware of her own feelings. Slowly, she acknowledged that a different world existed behind her "all together" facade. She ventured into the inner world of feelings where the light seemed less bright and the answers were not clearcut. This was an area of Jane in which efficiency was not a virtue, Control didn't help and performance was irrelevant.

Reluctantly, Jane realized that before she could have a different life experience, she would have to recognize her feelings as they currently existed. Acknowledging her vulnerability came slowly. Over several months Jane recognized her very young inner Child who didn't feel able to take care of herself. The Child had no control over her overwhelming feelings. The intensity of the Child's pain had led Jane, at an early age, to develop Control, the subpersonality who protected her against disappointment by telling her not to hope.

Jane imaged Control as a thick steel wall. Nothing could get through it or dent it. It also prevented the fearful Child from being seen or heard. Control led Jane to always present a polished appearance to others. Thus, she never looked needy (the Child was never seen). Jane imaged the Child to be untouchably isolated behind Control's wall. The impenetrable wall insured that the hurting, fearful Child wouldn't embarrass Control, but it also prevented the Child from healing. Her acquaintances would never guess that a needy Child existed.

Living behind that wall, the Child must have believed that no one would ever help her. In fact, no one could. Control prohibited any nurturing from penetrating through to the Child. The Child felt hopelessly alone and ignored behind that wall.

When we talked about Jane re-establishing a relationship with the Child, she hesitated. "There is so much pain; I don't want to feel it all." At the same time, Jane expressed a longing to be complete, a sense that some essential part of her was missing. She was trying to give herself something new from the outside (a baby) to make herself feel better rather than relating to that hidden inner Child and allowing healing to happen from within. Haven't we all been taught that taking in something from outside us—food, another person's attention, alcohol, TV—will make us feel better? The answer is always "out there" and we have to chase it. But Jane had done that long enough, and now she was willing to consider the inner journey I suggested.

So, Jane decided to become acquainted with her Child even though she was afraid. (After all, when had she let her feelings dissuade her when her mind was convinced of the efficacy of a certain decision?) She first looked to see what the Child was doing. "She's a quiet girl, playing by herself, wondering what she is supposed to do next." Her Child was so accustomed to being jerked around, following her "shoulds," that she couldn't easily tell Jane what she wanted. She exhibited no spontaneity. After watching her for many moments, Jane asked the girl what she was feeling. "I want you to love me," the Child said.

Jane realized that the girl was looking for acceptance. Again, she hesitated. Intuitively, Jane realized that accepting the Child involved a major commitment. She couldn't fool the girl as she could fool the adults in her outside world. The Child would know if she were truly receiving the acceptance she craved. Jane's experience had been that other adults were satisfied with a good show and she knew how to give them that. But she couldn't keep emotional distance and manipulate the girl. Commitment to that inner Child meant that Jane would have to let go of her habit of not feeling—her intellectualization, rationalization and denial. Commitment to that Child meant that Jane would experience everything that Child was experiencing. Opening herself to such strong feelings required Jane to develop a completely different orientation towards her inner world. She had lived since childhood with her unspoken decision to block off feelings. Could she totally reverse that decision?

Jane wasn't sure that she could or that she wanted to. She feared embarrassing herself in front of co-workers, crying in public and exploding with anger at her parents. Doing any of these things would upset the Control Jane had constructed in her world. She might lose all of her relationships and the respect of her acquaintances.

When Jane was expressing her fears, she realized that she was identified with Control. These were Control's fears. When Jane stepped back and remembered that she was both Control *and* the Child, she could allow herself to hear from each of them without having to take sides or to make a decision. She listened to them and heard this:

Control: I've built a comfortable life. I have a good job, earn decent money. My home is lovely and people who know me respect me. You might destroy all that I've worked so hard to build.

Child: I'm not comfortable. I'm not happy. I feel like you want to ignore me. You're afraid that I might smash your world.

Control: Yes, that's what I'm afraid of. I would prefer that you didn't exist at all. If I could kill you and be free of your depression, I would. I've tried.

Child: You have managed to keep me away from you. You've isolated parts of me. I don't make myself known very often but you can't kill this pain over not conceiving. It doesn't matter what you say, I ache because biologically I will never be a mother.

Control: You have your pets. The world doesn't need any more children anyway.

Child: (Doesn't say anything, but sobs hysterically).

Jane did not know how to move beyond this impasse. Her usual approach, intellectual reasoning, was useless. The fight between Control and the Child could not be resolved rationally nor would it disappear. This scene was replayed regularly with Control maintaining prominence until the intensity of the Child's feelings overwhelmed Control's defenses. Then there would be sobbing. When the crying had diminished, again Control was on top and the cycle continued. But Jane was willing to consider a re-orientation to her feelings. She knew there must be a way for her subpersonalities to relate to each other differently. She called upon an inner Adult figure to speak to Control.

Adult: While I would like to be perfect and to not have uncomfortable feelings, I do feel a huge lack in my life. The joy is missing. I want to be whole. I want to acknowledge the Child and listen to her.

Control: I will allow you to listen to her here in therapy, but I don't want you to share her with your friends.

Jane's Adult agreed to these conditions. With Control willing to temporarily withdraw, Jane invited the Child to speak about herself, but Jane needed a Caring Parent, a figure who could relate to the Child's feelings as well as the Adult's rationality. In her imaging Jane brought the Caring Parent and the Child together. The Child was slow to speak. She whispered so that the Parent had to strain to hear her:

Child: My feelings are so big. I can't feel all of them all by myself.

Parent: I know. I'm here with you.

Child: But you won't stay long.

Parent: I'll be here with you as long as I can. When I have to go, I promise I will return. I won't ignore you.

Child: I'm going to die. I can't stand these feelings.

Parent: Let me hold you. I'm here.

Child: The pain will kill me.

Parent: I'll protect you. No one will take away your life. I love you and I will watch over you.

Child: I'm afraid.

Parent: I know. Your feelings scare you. They're big and they're awful. But I'll be here with you while you feel them. Just look up at me every once in a while and remember that I'm here holding you. I won't let go of you.

Child: Please don't leave me. I can't make it on my own. I need you.

Parent: I understand. I'll be here for you as long as you need me.

Child: What if you have to go?

Parent: I will be back. I won't leave you on your own for very long. You're too little to survive without my protection and I will protect you. So, just go ahead and cry all you want and hurt until the hurt is gone. I'll be here.

Child: Don't go away. I need you.

Parent: You have me.

Jane/Caring Parent listened to the Child talk about her overwhelming fear, loneliness, alienation, and self-doubt. The Child became aware of, and grateful for, the Parent's concern. As she cried in the Parent's arms, she healed. After an hour of sobbing with fear and alienation, the Child felt stronger and closer to the Parent who didn't abandon her. This experience was repeated frequently for weeks.

As the Child realized that she wouldn't be silenced again, her loneliness changed. Loneliness was the word the Child used to describe her feelings when she couldn't make contact with the Caring Parent part of Jane. Jane had involved herself in all kinds of groups but her loneliness had not healed just by contact with other people. It was only when the Parent welcomed the Child with concern and a willingness to listen, that the Child felt relief from her loneliness. Gradually, her alienation disappeared and her self-doubt was eliminated. As she grew to know that her feelings and vulnerability were safe with the Parent, the Child experienced acceptance. She wasn't really so terribly needy; her vulnerability was the same as that which every other human experiences. Her feelings weren't terrifying or overwhelming. The Caring Parent certainly could handle hearing them; they must not be so horrible.

Jane hadn't developed her Caring Parent subpersonality prior to therapy because she had never had a model for that. Control had been modelled for her when she was a child, so she had related to her inner Child that same way. When I showed her another way of relating to her feelings, she could replicate that model and develop her inner Caring Parent. First, she had projected that figure onto me, the therapist, and then she owned her projection and found that part inside of her.

Jane wrote in her journal at this time:

However my Child feels in relation to the Caring Parent seems to be my experience in the world. When the Child feels safe with the Parent, I feel safe in the world. When the Child trusts that the Parent cares about her needs, I find myself trusting that others will treat my needs with respect. As the Parent nurtures the Child and protects her, I find that somehow I receive emotional and financial support, especially from Mike. Whatever goes on between my subpersonalities, especially those two, is reproduced in the outer world for me.

The most amazing change I've noticed has been in relation to Mike. When I started therapy, he didn't understand what I was looking for. He didn't want to participate directly and, after the first couple of months, I saw that the problems really weren't between us (at least originally), but in my way of thinking. (Not that he didn't contribute his share of craziness!) So I didn't pressure him to change or make him responsible for my happiness. I just focused on my inner world. (I never knew there was so much going on inside me!) I had always been responsible for keeping everything in order around me; I didn't realize that I was irresponsible about not attending to the confusion inside me. There was a whole world of hidden feelings there, feelings I really didn't want to see.

Specifically, my Child was the part of me that I had always, without awareness, hidden. When I was three or four, I couldn't do anything else but hide all that pain and outrage. Those fears about dying as a result of being abandoned were incredibly painful. Of course, I couldn't handle them when I was a kid. I didn't have my Caring Parent then. The abandoned Child was just left on her own to try to survive however she could. She couldn't, really, by herself, so I must have just removed myself from her, from those awful feelings which threatened to destroy me.

But I was describing my relationship with Mike. Unconsciously, I must have seen my abandoned Child in him many years ago. He's just like her in so many ways! He's angry and confused and in so much pain. When I first met him, something in me was pulled to him. I didn't know what it was—certainly, relating to him was difficult; he just would not do what I knew was good for him! I tried so hard to get him to straighten out. The hassles we had!

But in Al-Anon, and especially in therapy, I learned where my real responsibility lay—with that Child inside. I hadn't even realized I had a part of me like her.

So I started to do for her what I had tried to do for Mike. Just being with her was so painful! I hated experiencing all those old feelings—the fear and the desperation. But that's what having a relationship with someone is about, feeling whatever they're feeling with them. So I did it. I could only share her pain by finding the part of me that wasn't needy, that had an inner source of strength. All these years when I've acted so strong it was a cover-up; I was pretending. I didn't even know there was another way to live! I thought that since life was hard, I had to be tough, too.

I realized by listening to the Child that what I was missing was gentleness. That's always what I've loved about Mike. He's outrageous and embarrassing, but there is such a large part of him that is tender and sweet. Now I see how much I needed that in my life and how I wanted him to give it to me.

So without knowing it, I had made an unspoken agreement with him—I would take care of his needs for worldly security and he would provide me with the feelings I had lost. But the more intense his feelings were, the more I tried to control them and him. That's how I had always handled my own feelings. It was only when I learned a different way of relating to feelings in therapy that I could have a different relationship with Mike. Sometimes I marvel that our marriage could have survived all those tumultuous, chaotic years. We were kids when we got together and committed ourselves to each other. We didn't know what we were doing. Or did we? Actually, we couldn't have been more perfect for each other. That's why we drove each other nuts!

As my Caring Parent introduced gentleness into the relationship with the Child, I must have changed in relation to Mike, because he is more sensitive and more responsible towards me now. I let him live his own life without (too much) interference from me and he does just fine. He's had some blows, but he recovered from them and learned his lessons. He seems to be experiencing a shift in his inner relationships between his Demanding Child and his Responsible Adult. When I finally got out of his way, his

> Responsible Adult strengthened and related to the Demanding Child out of that strength. In the past, I had prevented that relationship from developing by always overwhelming his Adult. I could be more responsible, sooner and faster, so his Responsible Adult didn't have a chance.
>
> When I backed off and related to my own hurting Child instead of to his, he could develop more balance inside of himself. And he seems to be truly pleased with himself for doing that. He's more independent and self-confident and his job performance is more reliable than ever. He's apparently enjoying his stability even more than the thrills of previous years. He acts more whole and more adult. Coming from that strong place, he has more support to offer me and seems glad to do so.

Jane and Mike grew much closer through this experience of redefining their positions in the marriage. Their earlier roles, his Demanding Child and her Rescuer, which seemed to promise safety for each of them were, in fact, restricting them individually and together. By relinquishing total identification with one subpersonality, both Jane and Mike expanded their ways of being alive individually, with each other and with the world.

Jane's experience of herself in relation to everyone else reflected the harmony she felt when she balanced the relationships among her subpersonalities. She found that she did live in an outer world that was supportive when her inner world figures supported each other, that life really wasn't so hard and that she didn't have to be so tough. If she were feeling alone, as if no one would help her, she looked inside to see if her Parent were willing to help her Child. She learned to listen to herself. Jane began to trust that the world was a safe place to express her needs, and to believe that her needs could be met.

Her belief about having to deny her needs had changed. By recognizing her own needs, listening to them herself, having her Parent verbalize them for her Child and noticing others respond to her, Jane experienced true power. Early in life she had surmised that power came from erasing needs, cutting off her vulnerability. Now she found that her power lay in recognizing all the parts of herself, listening to them compassionately and responding to them.

A year after therapy ended I visited Jane in her home. She and Mike had just adopted a baby boy and were thrilled. They cooperated with each other as partners and supported the child from their abundant caring. Obviously, Jane's Control could not predominate with a newborn, but now that was not a problem for Jane. She enjoyed the surprises that necessarily came when sharing life with a baby.

She told me that after our work together had ended, she realized that she had wanted a child to replace her lost inner Child. Allowing the inner Child to surface had been far too threatening and, in her denial, she was hoping she could somehow recover that part of her life vicariously through a baby. When she committed herself to relating to her own Child, her desperate need for a baby vanished. She still wanted to be a mother but no longer was frantic.

When her wish for a child assumed normal proportions, when it wasn't based on denial or fear of her own feelings, it was fulfilled. Jane had experienced a unity and congruence in the world around her which precisely correlated with her unconscious subpersonalities' relationships and needs. "The universe wanted me to handle my own problems first before I could move to the next stage in my life. When I did, my wish came true!"

༻ ༻ ༻ ༻ ༻

How do you treat your Needy Child?

_____
_____
_____
_____

Do you ignore his/her needs? Do you indulge them?

_____
_____
_____

Do you tell yourself that other people's wants are more important than your inner Child's needs?

_____
_____
_____
_____
_____
_____
_____

Describe your Controller in terms of what s/he says to you and how s/he wants you to act:

_____
_____
_____
_____
_____

If it were up to your Controller, what image would you project?

_____
_____
_____
_____

If your Child were to be seen as s/he is, what image would you project?

_____
_____

Listen to your Controller and your Child having a dialogue. What do you hear?

_____
_____
_____
_____
_____
_____
_____
_____
_____
_____

Now have that same dialogue between the Child and a gentle Caring Parent.

_____
_____
_____
_____
_____
_____
_____
_____
_____
_____
_____
_____

Exercise

Imagine yourself sitting and watching a glass elevator. The elevator is on the level above you but is descending. Inside the elevator is your Child. As the elevator descends notice the Child's feet and lower legs. *(Pause.)* Then notice the upper legs and torso. *(Pause.)* As the elevator continues to descend notice the Child's upper body, arms and head. *(Pause.)*

The elevator reaches your level and stops. The doors open but the Child remains in the elevator. Notice the facial expression, the body posture, the breathing of the Child. *(Pause.)* Have the Child verbalize a statement about him/herself. *(Pause.)* Slowly the elevator doors close and the Child is carried to a higher level.

Continue watching. Again the elevator descends. This time your Parent is in it. Notice the Parent's feet, lower legs, upper legs, manner of dress, torso, arms, neck and face. *(Pause.)* The elevator doors open. Notice the body posture, facial expression and breathing pattern of the Parent. *(Pause.)* Have the Parent make a statement about him/herself and just listen. *(Pause.)* Again the elevator doors close and the figure is carried up to a higher level.

Continue watching. This time the elevator descends with both the Child and the Parent in it. Watch as the elevator approaches your level. See the doors open. *(Pause.)* Notice the body postures of the two figures. *(Pause.)* Notice if they are touching each other or interacting in any way. *(Pause.)* Notice the facial expressions of each figure. *(Pause.)* Have the Child turn to the Parent and say something, express a feeling, ask a question or anything else the Child wants. S/he may communicate the message verbally or non-verbally. *(Pause.)* Notice how the Parent received the Child's message. *(Pause.)* Does s/he respond? *(Pause.)* How? *(Pause.)* Does the communication between them continue? *(Pause.)* Does the Parent ask the Child for something? *(Pause.)* Notice their relationship as they interact. *(Pause.)* What seems to be the feeling tone between them? *(Pause.)* Have their communication continue as long as they want. *(Pause.)* When they conclude, notice if they touch. *(Pause.)* What is each feeling? *(Pause.)* Have the elevator doors close and the elevator ascend. Watch the two of them until they are no longer in view. What is happening in your body now? *(Pause.)* How deeply are you breathing?

Describe your imagery:

___

What did you notice about the Parent?

___

The Child?

Their relationship?

How is this dynamic enacted in your life and relationships?

When do you identify with your Parent?

How do you act then?

What do you appreciate about your Parent?

When do you identify with your Child?

How do you act then?

_____
_____
_____
_____
_____

What do you appreciate about your Child?

_____
_____
_____
_____
_____

What do the Parent and Child want from each other?

_____
_____
_____
_____
_____

What is your reaction to your imagery?

_____
_____
_____
_____
_____

Relationships are Reflections 5

At thirty-nine, Beth was a successful professional woman with a neat, well-groomed, business-like appearance. Everything about her was conservative—her dress, her manner, her speech, her hairstyle. She was basically attractive and added few "frivolous touches" to enhance her natural good looks. She used very little make-up and wore traditional dress styles, usually in black or navy. She spoke in softly modulated tones, but her forehead was often furrowed and her shoulders held high. Her body bespoke tension.

Beth said that she could handle herself competently and assertively in business contacts with men but that she felt frustrated in personal relationships when her vulnerability and dependency were involved. She stated that she wanted to be with a man who understood her, who was sensitive to her feelings.

Her speech was planned and focused, demonstrating clear, analytical thought patterns. She described her problem, the solutions she had tried, and what her reactions to the (unsuccessful) outcomes of those trials had been. She organized her thinking about her feelings in the same way she organized her business.

Her dark-rimmed glasses hid her eyes, which were surprisingly expressive when they were unshielded, reflecting emotions she did not express verbally. Beth tried to present a facade that was logical and analytical. Her thoughts were orderly and organized, her life planned. She still had dissatisfied feelings about her relationships but none of her "solutions" for her feelings had met her needs. It was as though she were operating on two parallel tracks. Professionally, her skills led her to accomplishment and acclaim. Personally, the same skills couldn't save her from loneliness.

Unconsciously, she was looking for balance; she wanted someone to compensate for her lack of emotional development. Her professional skills were of no value when feelings were involved. She had worked very hard for fourteen years and had achieved unusual success in her career. Now her work required less attention. The tension within her, pulling her towards relationship, grew, but Beth didn't know how to respond to her inner changes. When none of the faster, easier solutions she had first tried (new clothes, weight loss, a dating service) "worked," she considered therapy.

I realized when I sat with Beth that I was responding to two subpersonalities. On the one hand, her "bottom line" business approach, her dominant and most noticeable subpersonality, encouraged efficiency. "Time is money," her Business Woman seemed to be saying, "so let's not waste any." Her "let's take care of business" attitude contrasted greatly with the other side of her, the one who had led her into therapy. This subpersonality was like a Confused Child, retiring and afraid—the opposite of the Business Woman. The Child had no sense of being in charge in her life and, apparently, no understanding of her experience. She just seemed to stumble from one feeling to another. She didn't comprehend patterns in her relationships or how she was affecting others. Beth's brown eyes softened when she identified with the Confused Child and seemed cold and fixed when she was the Business Woman.

For several weeks, we focused on differentiating between these two figures. Beth knew the Business Woman well. She understood her values about logic, rationality, and smooth management. Indeed, she usually identified with the Business Woman. She thought of the Business Woman's approach to life as the only respectable way to live.

It took a shift in orientation for Beth to allow the Confused Child to be. The Business Woman was ashamed of this Child and tried to deny her existence. After weeks of therapy, Beth finally acknowledged that these Child feelings were a worthy and acceptable part of her. At that point, she allowed herself to open to the Confused Child and not to fight her.

The loneliness Beth had experienced provided the impetus she needed to examine her retiring subpersonality, the Child. After all, she had tried all of the Business Woman's suggestions repeatedly for years to no avail.

Beth had never given much prominence to the Confused Child and, consequently, she hardly knew her. The Child is the part of us involved in relationships. We engage in relationships in order to meet our needs for love and security—the same needs we had when we were born. We unconsciously structure our lives so that the way these needs were met in our young lives is repeated later in life. If dependency wasn't safe as a child, you need to help your hurt Child inside to recover by allowing the Child to fully feel the pain and by holding him/her while s/he cries. Only when the inner dependency needs are met, can a dependency relationship with another person work out well.

Beth had learned to think logically as a way of responding to her feelings when she was a child. Her parents were intellectually oriented and any problem which came up was subject to intellectual scrutiny. It was dissected, analyzed, discussed. Feelings, too, were subjected to this process. Then they were dismissed as being inferior to a more cognitive approach. Thus, early in life, Beth developed an analytical subpersonality and denied her Confused Child.

Now that Beth was accepting the Confused Child's right to her own existence, she could listen to her and know her. She recognized that the Confused Child's feelings had always intruded upon the Business Woman's well-organized plans.

The Confused Child spoke about matters the Business Woman didn't understand and couldn't appreciate:

Child: I am unbearably lonely. When Friday afternoon comes and I know I will be alone for two days, I'm frightened and sad. I don't know what to do. I walk around the park or go to the zoo and everywhere I see happy couples, men and women holding onto each other and laughing. It looks wonderful to me; that's what I want. But, I absolutely don't know how to make it happen. It isn't a task I can work on. Love isn't a job to be done. I want it desperately but I don't know how to get it.

Beth noticed how the Confused Child always seemed to feel overwhelmed and "done to," while the Business Woman was always ordered and in charge of her life. These two subpersonalities represented very different energies in Beth, two sides to her that seemed to have nothing in common besides living in the same body.

Two months after she had begun therapy, Beth met Sam. Within two weeks he had moved in with her. He provided the nurturing and understanding she had wanted. They talked for hours. He empathized with her in a way no other man had before. He attended to her wants. (Since he wasn't working, he had few distractions). He made her feelings the center of their conversations. Beth said that she was transformed. She had never experienced such fulfillment. Her Child was sure this was the Prince who would save her from her misery and confusion.

Several months later Sam disappeared as quickly as he had appeared. Beth was devastated. She again felt her old pain. "Why can't anyone love me? Have I ruined another relationship? What is so awful about me?" Her Child's confusion was reinforced and her feeling of inadequacy confirmed.

The Confused Child asked these questions repeatedly each time a relationship ended. Ever since she was an adolescent, this pattern had periodically led Beth into deep depressions. When she was dating someone, she was energetic, active, and hopeful that now her life would change. When each relationship ended she withdrew from everyone, spent most of her time indoors and gained weight. The Confused Child said, "If I can't be loved by a man, I'll give myself love by eating. It's one way not to hurt so much." As far as relationships in her life went (when she was open to them), Beth was either imagining herself about to be lifted out of her lifelong frustrations and disappointments, or plummeting down a dark hole, bereft of hope, overcome by ever-returning despair. The Business Woman usually avoided the whole area of relationships and focused on work. It was possible to be successful at work; relationships only led to disappointment.

The pain of losing each relationship had frightened Beth so much that she was cautious about meeting new men. After her Confused Child had been prominent in each relationship and each had ended so miserably, the Business Woman reasserted herself. At least she knew how to be successful. She would be so angry with the Confused Child for creating another debacle that she would resume prominence and block the Child out. So again, Beth's energy would be funnelled into work and the Child's needs for love pushed out of awareness. After several months of self-imposed isolation, with her Business Woman completely ignoring the Confused Child, Beth's loneliness and need for companionship would again fuel the Child's restlessness. Then, using the Child's judgment, Beth would jump into a relationship with any man. The cycle would repeat. She had been at the jumping in point when she met Sam.

With Sam's departure, and after more than a year of therapy, Beth recognized her pain as partly being a panicky fear of death. Her Adult mind told her that she wasn't helpless, but her feelings seemed to come from an Abandoned Infant. That Infant thought that if her chosen source of nurturance (in this case, Sam) was not attending to her, she wouldn't survive. With this insight, Beth realized that she was experiencing more than the disappointment of losing another adult relationship. She was also reliving some earlier unresolved feelings. The Abandoned Infant was at the core of her Confused Child. The dependency and the disappointment in the relationship with Sam were similar to certain childhood pains of the past. The current situation reawakened the buried Abandoned Infant and her terrified feelings.

Previously, when these painful feelings of abandonment had arisen at the end of relationships, Beth had always pushed them away. She had felt afraid and overwhelmed by their intensity. Her Business Woman would take over and the wound would be buried, unhealed because the feelings had not been fully felt. But now, being older, feeling stronger in general, and having the framework for understanding her experience that therapy provided, Beth surrendered to her pain and allowed healing to occur naturally. After learning to identify her subpersonalities in therapy and becoming familiar with how feelings are processed, Beth was now willing to trust her experience. She allowed her feelings to guide her. She didn't squelch the voice of the Confused Child or identify with the Business Woman. She just allowed the Child to maintain prominence and the hurt feelings to flow as they would.

Beth sobbed through much of the first month after Sam's departure. She described nightmares which woke her at least once a night. She lost ten pounds; since she wasn't resisting her feelings, she didn't choose to eat unless her body needed food. She felt miserable but didn't fight her feelings. She trusted that she was healing.

As she spent time with her inner world and knew her moods more precisely, she identified the Critic, the subpersonality who, she now realized, had influenced her for years. The Critic motivated the development of the Business Woman. It was the Critic's angry admonitions that the Business Woman responded to. When she could differentiate it, Beth recognized that the Critic's voice was loud and punishing. As Beth listened to the Critic's words, she recognized familiar condemnations and thoughts she had had about her own lack of value when each relationship had ended. During this time she wrote in her journal:

> Dealing with the Critic inside of me has been difficult. For years I didn't hear her voice clearly or recognize that her criticisms weren't true. I only knew I was depressed. I think that voice has been with me since I was young, but I've used food, alcohol, television or work to avoid it.
>
> I was displeased about my relationships, but they were just a reflection of my inner conflict with the Critic. That was where the real action was—inside of my head. Funny how that's always available to work on—I can't go anywhere without my head—and yet I try to avoid it. The Critic's words frighten me. There seems to be such power in them. The Critic scares me as though she were real and large and looming outside my body, threatening to hurt me. The danger seems great and imminent. The power seems not to be mine, but to belong to an enemy. She seems to be something autonomous inside of me which isn't me, and yet, she obviously *is* a part of me. I just can't get rid of her or integrate her.
>
> The Critic wants to kill me. She hates me, disparages me, and wants to hurt me any way she can. She tells me that no one loves me and that no one could ever love me because I'm such a horrible person. She tells me I'm fat and repulsive, that no one could stand being around me. She points out mistakes I make and ridicules me for them. So, of course I've wanted to avoid the Critic. I guess I hoped a lover would silence that voice forever, but it never worked. I couldn't avoid her.
>
> I guess the Critic-Child interaction is the "primary relationship" inside of me which isn't working—a prototype for all my external relationships. There's no hope of anything going smoothly outside my body until I deal with the Critic. No one can save me from her.

The Critic is as real a person as anyone I can see or touch. I hear her voice when I am still. I know when to listen for her by noticing my behavior. If I start to do anything compulsively—eating, working, exercising—I know the Critic is at work and I am trying to block her out. My anxiety about being alone is a sure giveaway that I am afraid of being with her. Such a tyrant to have attached to me!

I can't really escape the Critic, although I've tried to tell her off and take control. Since that didn't work, I'm going to call upon an Adult part of me to listen to her:

Adult: I can feel how angry you are. I know you hate me.

Critic: You're right. I do. Wouldn't anyone?

Adult: Some people don't. Some like me.

Critic: They don't know you the way I do. If they really saw you in your truth instead of that caring, compassionate act you put on, they would treat you the same way I do.

Adult: Maybe. But some of them have seen me at my worst and they've never said to me the things you have. I want to die after you've spoken to me.

Critic: That's because I tell you the truth. You deserve to be dead.

Adult: (What can I say to that? She's my enemy and wants to stay that way.) Critic, you are so angry. You must be very hurt. No one has treated you very well if you treat me this way.

Critic: I know what you're trying to do and it won't work. Sure, I've been alone all my life. That's how life is. You're a sissy believing it's otherwise. You're just too weak to make it.

Adult: You seem very strong to me. How did you become so strong?

Critic: Through hurting and then realizing that I had to be strong. If I didn't get strong, I would be just like you—a wimp—always simpering, falling apart at the slightest blow. And I wouldn't live that way. You may not have standards for how you appear to others, but I do and I won't conduct myself in such a needy fashion.

Adult: No, you've never appeared needy or wimpy to me.

Critic: Well, I'm not. I can't allow that. I can't afford to think only about my feelings. I have work to do and things to get done. I want to be a grown-up in this world so I act like one.

Adult: You do appear to be grown up.

Critic: And don't try to dig any deeper. That's all there is.

Adult: I try to appear grown-up, too, but I still have needs.

Critic: That's because you're such a wimp. You've got to stop thinking always about your needs. I've shut down my needs. I can't allow them to exist so I just get rid of them. They don't exist anymore.

Adult: Never? Sometimes at night don't you want to be held?

Critic: If I do, I read a book or get busy with something.

Adult: Have you ever had anyone really love you?

Critic: It doesn't matter.

Adult: It's always mattered to me.

Critic: I can't afford the luxury of wallowing in my feelings like you do.

Adult: I do give my feelings top priority. And I understand how it wouldn't fit for you to do that. I would like to get to know you. You've obviously done some thinking and have worked out your life in your own way.

Critic: And if you'd listen to me, you could do the same thing.

Adult: I'm listening.

Critic: You've fought me so hard all of your life, but I haven't noticed that you've done so well. I can't see that you've found a secret that I haven't. You won't let go of your belief that you can have your feelings and still be loved and taken care of. I know that no one is going to take care of you. You might as well give up hoping and trying to make it so.

Adult: Did you want to be taken care of at one time?

Critic: Sure, but I got over it. It's too painful to keep re-hashing that neediness the way you do. I couldn't put up with that much pain. It interferes with my efficiency.

Adult: It probably scared you, too.

Critic: I don't remember feeling scared, but I didn't want to live that way, so I just made up my mind and I changed those feelings.

Adult: Mind over feelings.

Critic: Yes, and it works.

Adult: Do you overeat or stay busy?

Critic: What's that got to do with anything?

Adult: Don't you see that they are related?

Critic: Efficiency and eating are two different things.

Adult: Sometimes, do you feel more cravings to eat than at other times?

Critic: Are you trying to get into my head now? If I feel like eating more sometimes, it's just physical. Don't introduce all that psychological garbage.

Adult: I respect all the things you've been able to get done. Certainly your efficiency has paid off and been recognized.

Critic: Right. So when are you going to get with it?

Adult: I don't know if I can function that way. You're just very different from me. And your way works fine for you, but some how I can't make it work for me. So, I will accept and acknowledge that you have your answers and I will accept me and keep looking for mine. I may always be searching.

Critic: If that's how you want to live... I don't know why anyone would want to live that way, always struggling. Why not just settle it and get on with the business of life?

Adult: I don't know how to answer that question. I just have to do what comes from inside me. I can't cut myself off from my needs and still be me, be alive, do what I have to do. Maybe we are each doing what we have to do but we are going about it differently.

Critic: Maybe. I don't understand you and I'm not really interested. Just don't come crying to me when you're in pain. If you've chosen to continue feeling your feelings, you will feel pain sometimes too, so don't expect that I will solve that for you.

Adult: OK, you've got a deal. I hope we can still talk sometimes. I admit I don't understand you and I don't expect you to understand me, but I think I would like to continue knowing you.

Critic: I'll be here. I just wish you'd take care of yourself.

Beth's Critic, a subpersonality she had formed unconsciously when she was a child based on childhood impressions of successful adults, was now her own internal living figure. The Critic, modeled on Beth's parents, had all the same qualities as the Business Woman—rationality, logic, clarity and lack of emotion. The Business Woman was just a specific form of the Critic which Beth found useful in her outer life. The Critic had tried to silence the Child's feelings and had dominated Beth by encouraging Beth's identification with the Business Woman. Beth had always experienced an intense inner conflict between her Critic and her Child but due to the Business Woman's prominence and her denial of the Child,

Beth was unaware of what her tension reflected. It hadn't seemed that there was another part to her other than the Business Woman— there were just unexplainable depressions and weight gain. She had thought that truly the Business Woman was all there was to her. Now she could clearly identify her Child's needs and hear her Critic's voice. Listening to the Critic kept Beth from being overrun by her. The Critic was only one subpersonality, a powerful one formed early based on her identification with her parents, but nevertheless only one part of her.

Beth found that she had to offer the Critic exactly what she (Beth) wanted to receive: acceptance. By allowing the Critic to be angry with her and by listening to that anger, Beth had formed a relationship with the Critic. Knowing the Critic involved being able to see her characteristics clearly. Just as intimacy with another person requires that we respect each other's separateness and boundaries, so does intimacy between subpersonalities. We need to know who is operating inside of us. Getting to know one subpersonality is like getting to know any person. Each has a history, her own values, and her own way of thinking.

When Beth's Adult and Critic were talking and listening to each other, the Child didn't get depressed. As long as they could talk and listen to one another, the force of the punishment from the Critic was reduced. Like an intrapsychic United Nations, with more talk there were fewer battles.

Beth's angry Critic didn't disappear. She was still aware that the Critic was active when she felt depressed, unloved and alone. At those times her Adult intervened for the passive Child and would listen and talk with the Critic. After several months of internal conversations, she recognized that it wasn't only the Critic who was angry. The Child was also upset.

Adult: I feel intense anger. Who is there?

Child: When you didn't say anything to my co-worker, Kim, to stop her from hurting me, my feeling of being powerless returned.

You are the voice through which I have power. If you don't speak for me I am powerless. I need you to protect me and to define my limits for others.

Adult: I was caught off guard last week. I will be prepared next time. I tried to protect you with Julie last month. I think your voice came through too much, too loudly.

Child: But at least you tried to protect me. I knew you heard me and acknowledged me. You were supportive of me. If you listen to me and are supportive and don't try to make me disappear in your bowels, I don't feel rage. It's you I react to, not Julie, or Kim or anyone else out there. They are just being themselves, but you won't let *me* be *myself*. You seem so concerned about making space for everyone else to be, but you squelch *me*. Why do I have to be sacrificed so that everyone else can be happy? Why do you care so much about them and apparently nothing about me? I won't allow you to ignore me. I am truly dependent upon your voice.

Adult: I can see that now. I will lend my voice to your needs but you scare me with your intensity. I guess that's why I worry about what you will say to people. We need a Moderator so that we can communicate with each other and with the out side world, too.

Moderator: Adult, you have tuned the Child out for a long time because she had tantrums. Now she is more mature. She can explain herself and you can understand her. I want her to be heard. I want to insure that her anger is recognized, In the office, we all must consider with whom we will be speaking. Kim is young and doesn't know her own inner world. She is flailing. She may be near her bottom point, so we have to remember that her stress is already extreme.

Child: Are you forgetting about me?

Moderator: No, I just want you to understand the situation you are going into. There are considerations other than your needs. We've seen what happens when you think only of your needs. I am aware that in the past the Adult has concentrated on others and excluded you. I can understand why you would be tense when you hear me talking that way, too. I want to take care of you, but I want to be your intermediary with others, also. I can't totally give in to you. I hear your concerns and I will respect them, but I will respect the others' needs, also. Kim, as a person, has a need not to be belittled or hurt. She is projecting onto everyone. It's obvious that she isn't solid. However, she is still responsible for her behavior. We will have to let her know her limits and what is unacceptable. I will do that. She has intense energy, but no focus or adult understanding. I will offer her a channel for directing her energy and I will protect you.

Child: OK, just don't forget me.

Moderator: I promise I never will. When I am in charge I want to hear your voice. But I will have the last word. I will own the needs you present to me and I will commit to staying open to you. I will help your feelings find a form which will be heard and which won't increase your isolation.

Child: OK, I don't completely trust you yet, but I will give your proposal a chance.

Beth's Moderator, an impartial mediator, reclaimed the Child's needs and expressed them through her own voice. The Moderator had not been a prominent part of Beth up to that point in her life. The struggle between the Critic and the Child had intensely consumed most of Beth's energy so that she couldn't detach from their passion. She had identified first with one and then the other. But the Moderator was not overwhelmed with emotion, nor was she simply a compromise between the Critic and the Child. She was a separate figure, more objectively analytical than either the Critic or the Child and committed to insuring their survival together. She didn't judge or take sides. She realized who was present and listened to each of them.

Beth's Critic wasn't committed to an ongoing relationship with the Child. That's why the Child looked outside of Beth for a man to give her the emotional support she wasn't receiving within. But no man she met was ever committed to an ongoing relationship with the Child, either.

Relationships show you which subpersonalities inside of you need attention. Whatever causes you difficulties in relationships reflects an inner relationship that isn't working well. If you are not feeling listened to by your lover, a prominent subpersonality isn't listening to your Child.

There was no way Beth could share a gentle, caring relationship with another human being until that relationship inside her was gentle and caring. It wasn't possible to side-step dealing with that inner relationship.

After a year alone, Beth said that she was glad that she had had the relationship with Sam. While dealing with her feelings about this in therapy, she had learned to allow her softer, feeling side to emerge. By surrendering to her feelings, she had learned to trust life and to allow it to guide her. She found that she could trust life to heal her even if she couldn't trust Sam to be with her.

Her Business Woman had believed that she had to provide for all of Beth's needs, that without her vigilance and consistent effort, Beth would suffer. By allowing her Child prominence, Beth surrendered to the life process. When she wasn't controlling everything she did and felt, she felt her feelings and then found that life was providing for her needs. No longer did she need her Business Woman's structure and intense focus. By going through her feelings and feeling them, instead of denying or controlling them, she found that her own process healed her. Her pain diminished naturally. By trusting and surrendering, she could allow herself to experience this healing process. The wounded Child had tried to get what she needed—love and understanding from others, but by the very fact of her woundedness the Child's efforts were doomed. A wounded Child is always primarily concerned with protecting herself. She may want to receive love but her fear of feeling hurt won't let her do it. Instinctively, she defends herself. That's the only way a hurt Child can think.

When the Moderator was willing to relate to the Child, the Child's hurts and wants and feelings could be heard. The Moderator could be with her while she cried and could offer her the attention she needed.

Men had treated Beth the way her Critic treated the Child. But when her unconscious dynamics changed—when the Critic was no longer hurting the Child and the Child was no longer defending herself—Beth's experience with men changed, too. After a second year alone, Beth wrote to me to announce her engagement. When she didn't need a man to "make her life OK," when she was comfortable with her internal interactions, her unconscious drew a caring man to her. The more experience she had receiving gentleness from a subpersonality within her, the more certain it became that she would receive gentleness from outside her.

Relationships with friends, a lover, or a mate are not mysterious, unknowable affairs. Love is not blind. There is reason and pattern to our experience. We do what we must, act out what our subpersonalities require. There are no errors or meaningless coincidences. Whatever we feel is necessary. It helps us to know our inner worlds better. The path to harmonious relationships lies within us.

If you are involved in a conflictual relationship, look for projections of a subpersonality in you of whom you're not aware. If a mate is unresponsive, who in you doesn't respond to your Child's needs? If a friend is controlling, what part in you wants to limit the Child's feelings? If a lover is embarrassing to you in public, what subpersonality in you is immature?

Remember, it is no fair saying, "If only s/he were different, then I'd be satisfied." S/he is the way s/he is, so that you can see yourself in his/her mirror and take responsibility for your own inner world. If there are changes to be made, they need to happen inside you. The people around you aren't the cause of the problems in your life; they're just a reflection. Look at them and then look at yourself. Unconsciously, you're choreographing your own dance. If it's too painful or frustrating, you need to change the choreography, not the dancers. And you do that by looking and listening inside yourself.

❧   ❧   ❧   ❧   ❧

Who are your most active subpersonalities in terms of relationships?
_____
_____
_____

How do they interact?
_____
_____
_____
_____
_____
_____

How do they handle dependency needs (needs for love and relationship)?
_____
_____
_____
_____
_____

What does your Critic, or any similar subpersonality, say to you?

How does your Child respond to your Critic?

What happens when your Child meets a projection of your Critic in another person?

Relaxation

Spend several minutes doing the relaxation exercise on page 9.

Exercise

Before you start this exercise have a pencil ready. You'll want to write while you're receiving your imagery so as not to forget it.

Let an image of the two parts of you who conflict about relationships appear. One will be an "anti-relationship" subpersonality and one will be "pro-relationship." Don't think about these parts—just invite them to come and wait until you have a sense of who they are. They may take any form—human figures, animals, inanimate objects. Just watch whatever comes to you. *(Pause.)* When the forms of these two figures are clear, address one of them. Notice that figure's characteristics. *(Pause.)* Ask him/her/it to tell you his/her/its three highest values. Listen. *(Pause.)* Without interrupting your meditative state, gently write these values down and return to your imagery. Ask him/her/it what its goals and desires are. Listen carefully, and write what you hear. Ask this figure how its values and goals affect its relationships. *(Pause.)* Write down the answer. Ask it to finish the following sentences, and write down each answer: "I need . . ." "I want . . ." "I can't stand . . ." Thank that figure for speaking with you.

Now move on to the second figure. Notice the characteristics of this figure. Ask him/her/it what its three highest values are. *(Pause.)* Ask him/her/it what its goals and desires are. *(Pause.)* Write them down. Ask this figure how its values and goals affect its relationships. Listen carefully, and write what you hear. Ask it to finish the following sentences, and write down each answer: "I need . . ." "I want . . ." "I can't stand . . ." Thank this figure for speaking with you.

Have the two figures face each other and look at each other. Have one figure describe how it feels to relate to the other. *(Pause.)* Now give the second figure a turn to express the same thing. *(Pause.)* Write down their dialogue as you are hearing it. Have them each express their frustrations and needs. Allow them to continue interacting as long as they wish. Just watch and listen.

Thank them and tell them you will be back to talk with them later. Allow your imagery to fade.

Use this space to write down what you heard.

Listening to the Body

6

Ann was a nurse with curly blond hair and lively brown eyes. She bounced rather than walked and bubbled rather than spoke. Her small body seemed to percolate. In her late twenties, Ann was frequently mistaken for eighteen. She lived by her feelings and often felt caught in a whirlwind. However, her buoyancy masked an underlying constriction.

When she began therapy, she had difficulty articulating her goals. She was restless and dissatisfied but could not precisely identify a problem. Life just wasn't turning out the way she had always expected it would. She was doing the same things she saw her peers doing, but she felt like she was only "going through the motions." Nothing had much meaning to her and the anchor of traditional values seemed to weigh her down rather than ground her. "I'm living in ways I was taught to, but I don't really feel like I'm living at all."

Psychological thinking seemed natural for Ann. She could discuss her feelings and wants, but only to a point. Before she could experience a peaking of emotion and a consequent resolution, something in her tightened and the feeling vanished. She was left numb, feeling more dead than before. Then her attempts at liveliness were increased in a desperate effort to fight off the gradually engulfing numbness. She felt like she was "drowning in quicksand," and struggling for her life. But, as in quicksand, the struggle didn't resolve her frustrations; it only led her to sink deeper. She couldn't pull herself out of the increasing darkness.

Being extroverted, Ann was aware of how others responded to her and wanted to talk about that in therapy. An imbalance inside of her was obvious, but we approached her inner world through the outer. After all, inner or outer—both lead us to the same conflicts.

Ann had lots of dates, but was dissatisfied with the relationships after a few weeks. She understood that the men she met reflected parts of herself to her and she didn't like what she saw.

She noticed several patterns in her relationships. One type of man she was attracted to was young and exciting. He wasn't committed to a career or to a mortgage. He was seductive but inconsistent. These men would take her dancing or to parties with their friends. They were great fun. For two or three weeks. But when Ann wanted to know them better, to see deeper than the "good time" facade, they disappeared. What could these men be showing me about myself? Ann wondered. In several imagery sessions, we invited the young, seductive, inconsistent subpersonality in Ann to speak to us. We closed our eyes and breathed for a few moments. An image appeared to Ann of a teenage girl. She reported the following interaction:

Observer: Please tell me about yourself.

Teenager: I am you—your feelings and your wants. I can get men to love me. I want attention and so I've learned that the way to get attention is by listening, by getting men to talk about themselves and by showing only my sweet side.

Observer: Yes, I recognize you. You take over when there's fear and the Adult doesn't know what to do.

Teenager: I can manage to get through any situation by flattering people. I am good at knowing what they want to hear and giving it to them.

Observer: Something about that sounds uncomfortable.

Teenager: I'm just doing what will make people love me.

Observer: Does everyone love you when you do your "act"?

Teenager: Not everyone. With women, especially older women, it works well. With young men it will work well enough for them to love me for an evening or a week. We go to bed but they don't call back.

Observer: That must feel terrible.

Teenager: Yes. (Crying softly.) I don't know how to make any one love me for a long time.

Observer: You can't force love to happen, can you?

Teenager: No, and it scares me that I will always be alone. No one stays around. What's wrong? What should I do differently?

Observer: You're such a confused, hurt kid. Let me know you and be with you. I may not have any solutions for you but at least you don't have to do your act with me.

Ann realized that her Teenager was a Child with a teenager's appearance, doing adult things. The Child wanted to be loved. The Teenager thought of teenage ways of getting love. Love became a matter of manipulation, giving people what they wanted in hopes that they would then depend on her so much they wouldn't leave her. (Ann made the connection between this way of thinking and her choice of nursing as a career. How could a dependency relationship be acted out more precisely than with people who needed her so that they could survive physically?)

Obviously, Ann's Child/Teenager didn't have a sense of receiving love freely given. She couldn't accept the fact that some people wouldn't love her. The Teenager thought that if someone didn't love her, it was her fault and she could change it so that everyone would love her. She didn't want to relinquish her belief that there was an underlying rational logic to life—that what happened to her was a consequence of how hard she tried to be good. Circumstances had never proved this to be true, but she continued to try to make it true.

Ann understood that she was holding onto a childhood notion in her Teenager subpersonality. This Child/Teenager was relating to everyone she met as though they were parents to be pleased. And she continued to employ with everyone else the methods she had learned to please her parents—being focused on their needs and denying her own. That pleasing act had worked with her parents, but trying to get love from everyone else that way hadn't given her a stable, long-lasting sense of her own value and worth. She did receive approval for her act sometimes, from some people, but this merely perpetuated an unsatisfying cycle. In fact, this way of manipulating for love reinforced her belief that, as a person, she wasn't valuable. Her only worth came from what she could do for another. And so the cycle continued.

Another type of man Ann unconsciously attracted to her was initially solicitous. Then, after she became interested in him, he became distracted and withdrawn. He would forget dates or be an hour late. She felt like she had been picked up and dropped with no warning. She didn't understand what was going on in these men's minds; she just kept waiting for them. When they did appear she was pleasant and didn't mention her disappointment.

Ann's Adult felt impatient with her Child for tolerating such poor treatment. The Child seemed to be so needy! She was always making herself available to people—especially irresponsible men—and always being abandoned in the end.

Adult: How can you allow yourself to be treated so inconsiderately? It infuriates me to see how these men treat you and how you just accept it.

Child: What else can I do?

Adult: Yell, scream, kick them in the knee. Do something!

Child: (Whimpering.) I can't. I just can't. I can't take care of myself. I need someone to take care of me. That's what I always hope a man will do for me.

Adult: They never do, though, do they? So why do you still hope? Are you stupid?

Child: (Now crying.) I guess I am. Maybe the next man, if there is one, will love me.

Adult: Let's not talk about love. I don't think that's really what's happening here at all. I think it's dependency. You want someone else to take away your scared feelings and make you happy.

Child: (Brightening.) Sounds good to me!

Adult: Well, it won't happen. Your feelings are your life. You have to love them and embrace them and accept them.

Child: I'm too little.

Adult: OK, you exasperate me but I will have to care as much about you as I'm asking you to care about yourself. I'll take care of you. I can do a better job than any man can, anyway.

Child: (Warily.) What can you do for me?

Adult: I can be consistent. I'll always be sensitive to your feelings.

Child: You haven't been around for me before. Why will you be available now?

Adult: Because you're getting into painful situations using no judgment with men who don't care about you. I can't stand the pain anymore.

Child: You haven't treated me any differently from the way these men do. You expect me to be nice. You'd rather be with anyone other than me.

Adult: I know I've treated you insensitively in the past. I'm sorry. What I would like to do in the present and the future is to listen to your wants, but I want to be the one making the relationships in the world. You won't have to go to any one else; I will take care of you. I can't trust that you will handle yourself appropriately with others so let me respond to you and I will handle the relationships with others.

Child: Well, if you are always available to me . . . But, wait, what about when I want to be held?

Adult: I'll hold you. I'll listen to you. I'll let you cry or be angry.

Child: It's not the same.

Adult: Right! I don't want our relationship to be the same as the awful relationships you've been getting into. I want it to work out better. I realize that it's been my disregard for your feelings that has led you to approach other people to get what you wanted. It has never worked out so I will sincerely commit to you that I want a relationship to work out between us.

Child: Well, that's a commitment I've never heard from a man.

Adult: See? Already you're seeing how much I care.

Ann's Child, with her need for love, had finally made contact with her Adult. Previously, the Adult had ignored the Child. When the Child wanted attention, she was on her own, devising her Child means to gain it from others. The Adult hadn't contributed her Adult judgment to implement reasonable behavior. The two subpersonalities had always worked separately. This was the first conversation in which the Adult had acknowledged the Child's wants and treated them seriously. Now the Adult had promised to contribute her skills, to cooperate with the Child in meeting her needs rather than ignoring her. As long as the Adult ignored her, the Child was certain to be frustrated. As with all of us, the Child tells us our wants and needs, but the Adult tells us how to meet the needs successfully. So, cooperation between the two is necessary if the Child is to be happy and the Adult satisfied.

In her commitment to focus upon the relationships among her subpersonalities in her inner world, Ann decided to stop dating for awhile. She had gathered information by looking at her experience with others and was now ready to apply what she had learned to the ongoing drama within. She had developed a rhythm—first focusing on the outside to gather data and then focusing inside to use the data to clarify inner dynamics.

From her subpersonality conversations, Ann realized that she must listen to her needy Child and develop a strong relationship with her. That Child had never experienced a consistent loving relationship that wasn't built on service or manipulation. So her Adult decided to show her what that would be like. The Adult treated the Child with the same genuine kindness and caring that Ann gave to her patients. She checked inside with the Child to ask what she wanted each day. Anytime Ann felt off-center, she knew the Child needed her. She began to recognize the cues that her Child gave her when she wanted attention. When Ann was restless and couldn't concentrate, her Adult asked her Child what she wanted. When the Child was satisfied,

Ann could continue with her Adult world and work. If the Child were not satisfied, Ann would have to stop and care for her first. Providing anything her Child needed became the Adult's priority.

Ann saw the failure of her Child/Teenager to mature. They were stuck back in a reality which didn't exist any longer. Her parents had both been young professionals during Ann's early childhood. They provided all of the "things" any child could need but didn't stay around long themselves. They were very busy and quite active in their careers. From relating to them, Ann learned to be undemanding emotionally. She didn't present them with any needs; they didn't have time for that. If the world couldn't handle her needs, she just wouldn't have any. So, she learned to adapt to her parents and used that same method to deal with the world.

In this environment, some subpersonalities were encouraged to grow, while others were severely limited. Her self-reliant-acting Little Adult was given prominence, while her dependent Wimp was pushed aside. Her take-charge-of-the-situation Leader received approbation, while her frightened Recluse receded. From the very subtle conditioning of her parents' attention when she was strong and withdrawal when she was needy, Ann learned the act that would be rewarded. This conditioning process was totally unconscious on her parents' part and on hers. She learned to value some parts of her and to disregard others.

Subpersonalities, when they are ignored, may remain hidden for a very long time, but they will always resurface in one form or another. They never disappear. Implicitly, they demand to be dealt with. Ann's need could remain out of sight for years, but it wasn't quietly dormant. The natural energy it carried had to be distorted to keep it unconscious, and this resulted in anger.

It seemed to her Child that her biological parents weren't permitting part of her to exist. It was an arrangement the Child, because of her dependency, had to accept and adjust to. Whatever the caretakers want is how things will be. As a baby, Ann assimilated the unconscious expectations of her parents and unknowingly formed pleasing subpersonalities to collude with them.

Underneath her pleasing act, however, Ann was resentful. She could not make her parents love her the way she wanted no matter what she tried. She simply could not turn them into the attentive parents she would have preferred. Her manipulations, designed to achieve these ends and avoid pain, had failed. However, these manipulations continued. In spite of having evidence that "being nice" didn't bring acceptance and intimacy, Ann continued this pattern with the world as she grew. She still was fighting a battle that had already been lost. In order to see her current reality accurately, Ann realized that she needed to release the childhood anger she still felt towards her parents for their inattention. She had continued to feel like a lonely Child and to view the world as unresponsive to her needs.

During this time in therapy, Ann happened to notice a picture of herself at three weeks old. She was so tiny! She was struck immediately with the thought: I am no longer that baby, but I am holding onto feelings that started with her. She understood how desperately that baby must have wanted and needed attention, but she realized she did not have to identify with that baby or with that desperate need. In fact, now as an adult, she did not need anyone's attention to survive. She could take care of all of her physical needs. If no one loved her, she wouldn't die. She reconciled her feelings with her current adult reality.

She wrote about this reconciliation process in her journal:

> My Adult sits quietly for two or three minutes and breathes and relaxes and forgets about her own concerns. When she is genuinely able to be present with the Child, she asks the Child to come sit with her and tell her her feelings. The Child says she is scared. The Adult allows the Child to be afraid and doesn't fight

her or try to dissuade her. No matter what the Child feels, it is OK with the Adult. She stays right with the Child and holds her. The Adult accepts the intensity of all of the Child's feelings and lets them be, just as they are. When the Child has spent her emotion, the Adult uses her discerning mind to hear the beliefs from which those feelings sprang. Fear stems from the belief that, "No one will protect me and I may die." Loneliness stems from the belief that, "I am an unlovable person if I act just the way I feel." Neediness stems from the belief that, "It's better to take care of others than to want them to take care of me. It's safer. They will keep me around then." Now that these beliefs are conscious, I can evaluate their relevance to my life now. My Adult can determine whether or not she wishes to continue adhering to these beliefs or to release them.

Ann discovered that the Child was living with these unconscious beliefs:

> I have no value unless I serve others.
> I will be abandoned if I am honest about my
>   feelings and my needs.
> It's not safe to trust anyone.
> I can't have what I want.
> My needs are insatiable.
> I am very angry.
> Only those people who depend on me will
>   stay with me.

As she went through this process, carefully and precisely elucidating her unconscious beliefs, Ann let them go. She couldn't separate from them until she was aware of what she was holding onto. As they became conscious, her responsibility in maintaining her own reality became clear. She had been unconsciously proving the basic beliefs which had structured her life. If the unconscious belief were: "I can't have what I want," Ann could see that the men she chose to have relationships with couldn't meet her needs. By putting energy into relationships with these men, she proved that belief. If the belief were: "I will be abandoned if I am honest about my feelings," she could recognize that unconsciously she had chosen to relate to persons who would certainly abandon her. Through these beliefs, her Child gave understanding and meaning to her experience. Whatever she felt and whatever happened to her were filtered through these beliefs. Any experience could be distorted to fit these unconscious "truths." If someone left her, it was because "I have no value." If she were unsatisfied in a relationship, it was because, "My needs are insatiable." She always referred back to these unconscious beliefs to explain her experience.

With her awareness of these dynamics, Ann could release them. She could see that dissatisfaction or abandonment were guaranteed in her choice of a partner. She couldn't change the men. So when they lived up to their natures, her Parent voice could say, "See, I told you it would happen. It's because...(insert any belief)." Thus, she always took responsibility for the failure of relationships by blaming her own behavior, not realizing that in order to continue adhering to her unconscious beliefs, she needed the relationships to fail. As she became aware of her self-defeating beliefs and behaviors, she could release her anger with her parents, for she didn't need them to be attentive parents any longer. She could accept them as the well-intentioned people they were without trying to change them into her image of ideal parents. After all, for the past twenty-five years, they hadn't been trying to kill her needs. She had freely assumed that job and was carrying it out quite well on her own! When she took responsibility for her inner, rule-administering Parent, she could re-focus her attention away from her biological parents to the true power source, her own Parent subpersonality. Her Parent subpersonality wanted to keep the Child safe, and so interpreted the Rules of the World for her. The Child clung to these rules and unquestioningly made them her beliefs. This process took place so subtly and so long ago that these beliefs became an unconscious foundation on which Ann built her life.

Ann's parents had loved her very much, but she was still unsatisfied as a baby. Now she didn't need her parents in that same way she did then and it was OK to say, "Yes, I was disappointed as a child, but now childhood is over." When the work of her inner Parent was made conscious, she could alter it. She realigned the distribution of power among her subpersonalities by doing so. **When the unconscious is made conscious, it loses its force.** When its words can be heard and scrutinized, their impact can be minimized. When Ann released those subtle feeling-squelching messages, she no longer resented her internal Parent or her biological parents. Thus, in a deep sense, childhood was over. Her Parent no longer had the power, and her Child was no longer dependent on an ungiving source.

Ann accepted herself and her independence. She had some needs, but she also had strength. She began to let the seductive and inconsistent men pass by. She knew they would be fun for a short time but that they offered nothing her Adult wanted. As Ann accepted her own inconsistent Teenager, she could know that subpersonality through the Adult's eyes. Her identification transferred more and more to the Adult rather than the acting-out Teenager. The Teenager assumed less prominence and influence and so, naturally, her interest in men who acted out her Teenager's values declined.

Nothing in Ann's life could assume greater importance than the Adult insuring the comfort of her Child. As her Child was happier, she asked for less and contributed to Ann's enjoyment and delight in everyday events. The Child didn't want to be a drain on Ann but when she was scared and needy, she couldn't do anything else. With Ann's attention she became less needy, appropriately trusting and generally happier. Instead of being a nuisance to Ann, she offered her a way of looking at the world which was creative and fun—a place to play and enjoy herself.

While gaining more perspective on her relationships internally and externally, Ann began to think about men as being projections of her masculine figure inside. The men she encountered must have similar characteristics to her inner masculine subpersonality. The thought made her shudder.

She decided to listen to her inner Male and to relate to him. She went through a process of self-relaxation, allowing her mind to become blank. She focused on her breath and invited her inner Male to show himself to her. She wrote in her journal:

> His name was Ralph. Ugh. I've always disliked that name. He's no pleasant sight, either. He's fat, unclean and retarded. I disliked him immediately. He knew it and didn't like me for it. So I realized that I would have to spend time with him. I sat with him at dinner and told him how to use silverware. He had no table manners, so I made some suggestions about keeping his mouth closed and his elbows off the table. He wanted to gulp his food, but I encouraged him to eat slowly and enjoy his dinner. The change in him was surprising. He appreciated the attention and responded to my suggestions. He knew he needed some education in living gracefully and took in everything I said. I felt like I was with a young man who hadn't had any social experience. (I've felt the same way with a couple of my boyfriends!) Ralph was ready to learn and was waiting to be acknowledged.
>
> *Next Day:*
>
> This morning when I was walking, I called to Ralph and asked him to be with me. When he came, he was different from last night. He was dark, physically very fit, and proud of his athletic body. As I walked, he sprinted back and forth. This time he was talking to me, educating me in areas he thought I had neglected. He was very sensual and talked to me about including the appreciation of the sensual in my life. He suggested that I do small things—take time to appreciate beauty around me, feel textures, be aware of subtleties. Oh, yes, and he said his name was Mr. Rolf. I thought he could add some nice touches to my life, including some deeper levels of awareness, so I could live more fully. He interested me; I wanted to know him better.
>
> *Next Day:*
>
> Today when we spoke, "Ralph" had changed again. In fact, he told me his name is Raul. He is Mexican and earthy. He loves

> women. He spoke to me about sexuality in gentle terms. He seems to understand just how hard that is for me so he doesn't push me or make fun of me. He did suggest that I try little exercises, like lying on the floor and feeling my sexual feelings. He was careful not to embarrass me or to push me faster than he knew I could go.
>
> He seems to know me precisely and to respect me, but to be very different from me. He owns all of those characteristics I don't consciously acknowledge—my aggression, my anger, my sexuality. He seems foreign yet familiar. I can't predict the way he thinks, but it doesn't surprise me. I understand him, but I haven't had his experiences. He is much more comfortable with his body and his instincts than I am with mine. Even though I've slept with men, I've done it for their approval, not really out of my body for sensual pleasure, but out of my head. It was another manipulation, a way of giving a man what I thought he wanted in order to keep him with me.
>
> Raul lives out of his insides. He isn't intellectual, yet he is very grounded. He moves over the earth like a sleek cat. He knows what is real, but is unconcerned with ideas. He is sure of himself and the world because he lives out of his physical nature. He can feel and see and he trusts his senses. He knows because he experiences. His body and its experience are his bases for making judgments and decisions.

This subpersonality in Ann functioned very differently from her Child, who had often been focused on others. Raul was anchored within himself and always looked inside himself to discover his wants. From knowing his wants, he decided on his actions. He lived by a natural cycle which excluded his intellect; he felt, then he acted. His feelings led him.

After several weeks Ann noticed that, although she wasn't calling upon a masculine figure as a distinct part of her, her behavior in general was different. Without effort, she was becoming assertive and self-protective. A major shift she noticed was that she was again becoming interested in sex. With her temporary withdrawal from dating, she had made a commitment to herself to be celibate. Now, her body seemed to be pulling her back to her own sexuality. She noticed more sexual feelings and, more surprisingly, she found herself willing to stroke her body. She began to enjoy sensual pleasure by herself and to be aware that her body was sensual.

She had been raised strictly and had never touched herself, but now her body wanted to be touched. She felt deep flows move within her. She was responsive to her own touch. She had not experienced this before.

As she spent time alone with her body, she learned to know it better. She listened carefully to what her body wanted and needed. She recognized fatigue which her mind had always ignored and pushed her through. She recognized specific desires for food.

Before this time, she had felt guilty or disgusted touching her body. Her mind had no need for her to listen to her body at all, and so, she hadn't until recently. Now, however, there seemed to be a freedom, an openness as though she had been released from a confining space. Her experience wasn't intellectual, but physical. With her freedom to relate intimately to her own body, she felt a whole world open to her. She embraced her life as truly her own and lived out of her body instead of by the rules in her head.

Now she realized how oppressed she had been by her intellect and by all the rules from her past. She understood that she was not living her own life with the aliveness and spontaneity which come from listening to the wants and needs of one's body and feelings. Previously, she had been imitating a set of rules and restrictions her Child mind had adopted to keep her safe with authority figures. Ann now viewed that Child, who wanted so desperately to be loved, with compassion. She really didn't feel that her life had been wasted, but that her Child had had to live as she did. Given her early experiences and decisions (to be good, to submit to authorities) Ann realized that her life could have gone no other way. Her Adult and Child grew together as they communicated and respected each other.

She had a sense of her life changing profoundly. She loved the Child, but it was time to identify with her Responsible Adult. She no longer lived in an obedient, submissive way, but chose the risks inherent in "living from within" her body. As she wrote in her journal:

> Living from within my body means that I am pulled, not pushed. My mind doesn't pressure, cajole or criticize. Rather, I am pulled, compelled by some deeper intuition. My image is of a rope coming out of my solar plexus that extends in front of me. I can't see where it is attached on the other end, but it draws me. I allow it to lead me into experiences which turn out to be perfect for me. In little ways, my intuition guides me through my days, gently tugging me to the left or to the right or encouraging me to be still. As I follow its lead, I am given gifts—an unexpected encounter, a beneficial coincidence. Whatever is pulling me on the long rope has an unerring sense of timing. When I go with it, I experience exactly what I need to, but what my mind, with its control, cannot predict. I can see now how my mind's control is good for some things—I need it when I'm pressing a straight crease in my slacks or when the accountant wants my tax information—but it can't help me in other ways. It isn't any good at living creatively or at celebrating. That's not its job. I have to listen to another part of me for that.
>
> This rope seems to connect me to a level of life where there's magic—a wonderland where everything is connected and flows together easily. I don't jump out of bed to go exercise, but instead rest and receive a phone call I value, but would have missed if I were "being good, doing what I should." There is an underlying order and pattern and flow to everything which I didn't experience when I was busy following my head's commands. It's not my head's fault; I asked it to keep me safe and it did that the only way it could—by using control. But when I don't need safety, I don't need control. Now I need aliveness and connection. That's what I look to my body/feelings/intuition for. I'll give my head a rest. It has worked so hard for me but now I'll let my body pull me. There's no effort to that! It just takes my letting go and being willing to follow. And I am!

Ann became increasingly spontaneous and less "careful" in defensive ways. She sought out fun times and people and reduced her working time. She began to see life as an adventure. She felt like she was given gifts and only had to be willing to receive them and experience her own feelings. Her sense of being loved expanded. Not only could she imagine being loved by individuals around her, but also that she had a place in the world, physical and spiritual. She knew in her heart that she was acceptable as a person and that anything she would hear from inside her was acceptable, also.

As she moved through the world easily, Ann recognized and enjoyed others who were also moving through the world easily. She no longer felt compelled to be with people who were depressed or unsuccessful. Formerly, her friends had functioned similarly to Ann when she was identified with the powerless, miserable Child. She recognized that this stance held no virtue, but was a defense against the fear of living her own life and risking rejection.

She understood living her own life to mean listening to all parts of herself, not only those parts adult authorities had rewarded when she was small. As she related to all the subpersonalities within her and didn't cut them off, she listened to their voices and knew their world. She understood how they felt and what they perceived and wanted. She cared for them responsibly as she understood them. She considered their suggestions. She also realized that they were parts of her life, not annoyances to be discarded. She came to experience her aliveness as she acknowledged the wants of each of her subpersonalities. She couldn't ignore any of them without hurting herself.

As she listened to each part and respected its needs, she found that she finished tasks. She had always had trouble completing small jobs, but now there were no pulls on her energy to distract her. None of her subpersonalities were pouting from neglect, so each contributed its energy when there was a job to do. If she did feel stuck, Ann would look inside and ask who wanted attention and then she would listen. She recognized that feeling stuck indicated that some subpersonality hadn't received the attention it needed.

Relating to her inner world became a priority and a commitment for Ann. She felt as though she had a new support system with members who already knew her very well. She learned to discuss plans with her group of subpersonalities and to listen to the response of each member before making a decision or undertaking an action. (Try it—it works!) She delighted in meeting new parts of herself and never knew who would respond when she journeyed inside.

Ann noticed that her subpersonalities changed over time and that some new ones appeared. She said that it reflected her maturing process. She realized that she had sacrificed true maturity in order to play roles she thought would earn approval. She developed a new definition of maturity—knowing and accepting her inner world with all of its subpersonalities.

❦ ❦ ❦ ❦ ❦

What have you done in your life when you wanted approval?

_____
_____
_____
_____
_____
_____

Which subpersonality do you think was motivating you?

_____
_____

Who is the most sexual subpersonality in you?

___

Does s/he have an adversary? Who?

___

Which of your subpersonalities is projected onto your partner in your love relationship(s)?

___

Which of your subpersonalities have been relegated to your unconscious (pushed away from you because you didn't want to see it) at one time or another?

___

Have you been ignoring some parts of you in order to be "mature"? Which parts?

_____
_____
_____
_____
_____
_____

Relaxation

Spend several minutes doing the relaxation exercise on page 9.

Exercise

Imagine yourself entering a room in which there are several figures seated at a table and one empty chair. Walk over and sit in the empty chair. Notice the table. (*Pause.*) What is its shape? What is it made of? (*Pause.*)

Notice quickly how many figures are seated at the table. (*Pause.*) Are they human, animal, plant, mineral, or something else? (*Pause.*) Turn and look at the figure on your left. (*Pause.*) Notice that figure's gender, body posture, facial expression, breathing or any other characteristics. (*Pause.*) The figure has a name tag on his/her left shoulder stating the name or label for the subpersonality s/he represents. What is on the name tag? (*Pause.*) Ask that figure to speak to you describing what s/he does for you. (*Pause.*) Have him/her tell you about a time in your life when s/he was prominent, controlling the action in your life. Listen. (*Pause.*)

When s/he is finished, focus upon the figure to his/her left. Again notice the gender, body posture, facial expression and breathing. (*Pause.*) Read that figure's name tag. (*Pause.*) Have that figure tell you what s/he does for you and when s/he was prominent in your life. Listen. (*Pause.*)

When that figure is finished, continue attending to each figure around the table, repeating the process. (*Pause.*) (Even if the figures are people you know, they still represent some part of you. If you are not sure which subpersonalities they represent, ask them. If you are still confused, let three adjectives come to mind describing the person. Those adjectives describe the part of you that person represents.)

After each figure has spoken, suggest that they discuss some issue of current concern to you. Notice who starts the discussion. (*Pause.*) Who dominates the discussion? (*Pause.*) Who is quiet? (*Pause.*) Which two figures interact most? (*Pause.*) Which are adversaries? (*Pause.*) Which are allies? (*Pause.*) Is any one a leader? (*Pause.*) Watch and listen. Notice how the conversation progresses.

Now you notice another subpersonality on the ceiling. That figure has always been there, but you haven't noticed him/her before. S/he has been watching everything that has transpired. S/he understands each figure at the table well. As they become quiet, s/he speaks to each figure in turn. S/he knows precisely what message each one needs to receive. Listen to what s/he tells each figure. (*Pause.*) After s/he has given each figure a message, the subpersonality on the ceiling has a message for you. Listen. (*Pause.*) What are you told? (*Pause.*)

Notice how the different figures interact after they have received their messages. (*Pause.*) Is there a resolution or a conclusion to the discussion?

Describe your imagery. What were the details of the room and the table? Describe each figure with its name tag and what each one said.

Describe the discussion. What was the topic?

Who dominated?

_____
_____
_____
_____
_____
_____

Who was quiet?

_____
_____
_____
_____
_____
_____

Who interacted?

_____
_____
_____
_____
_____
_____

Each of the figures represents a subpersonality. What part does each subpersonality play in your life?

_____
_____
_____
_____

What part of you is the subpersonality on the ceiling?

What were the messages that ceiling figure gave to each subpersonality and to you?

Healing Addiction 7

Even people who don't appear to be Good People are being Good People in their own minds. Have you ever met a Bitch or a Bastard? Why do you think s/he has given so much energy to that one subpersonality and has hidden the gentle and sensitive Child? Somehow in their lives it's been better to do that. Being good for them is being tough. All of us have every kind of subpersonality inside of us. Usually we think of Good People as having developed the "nice" subpersonalities but some Good People develop a different sort of mask. The Bitch or the Con Man or some other character predominates and hides the Hurting Child. The purpose of any kind of mask is to shield the inner vulnerability. This can be done by identifying with the Always-Available Helper, as well as by acting out the Cantankerous Curmudgeon. It depends in part on the environment. Whatever "worked" in living with the childhood authorities gets adopted as "the way to be," the subpersonality to be strengthened.

Nancy and Jeff sought marital counseling for increasing conflicts. They had been married for three years. Nancy was thirty and Jeff was thirty-six. Nancy had arranged the therapy appointment. They presented the appearance of an ideal couple in many ways. Both were attractive and pleasant.

Jeff's attire was casual but appropriate. At times he was charming and witty. There was a boyish quality to him that seemed to say that life was to be enjoyed and he knew how to do it. I suspected that many women found him appealing. When he related his history, he described many relationships and affairs before his marriage at thirty-three, thus confirming my suspicion.

Nancy, tall and slender, was more serious. Her brown eyes narrowed and she looked away as she discussed her concerns. She tried to describe precisely their disagreements and her feelings, but often expressed the dynamics of their relationship in abstract terms. "He is more likely to wait for me to suggest an activity and to want to be around me. He doesn't want to talk with me about my feelings but just to have me in the yard working near him. He holds me at an arm's length away from him. He won't let go of me and he won't bend his arm so I can move closer. He likes to be sure I'm around, but not too close."

She reported that their communication was unsatisfying for her, that she felt like there was a part of Jeff she "just couldn't reach." She stated that over the course of their marriage this had been increasingly true. When they were dating she felt "swept off her feet by his grand gestures"—a dozen white roses delivered to the office for her birthday, romantic champagne sails at dusk, beautiful personalized jewelry. He couldn't do enough for her. After their marriage, and increasingly as time passed, she described Jeff as "distant." He was frequently tired or preoccupied when she wanted to talk with him. She had suggested therapy previously but he had resisted the idea.

Now, he wanted them to have a child. Nancy would not agree to take this step with him unless they received help for what she termed their "lack of intimacy." Because he wanted a family, he agreed to join her in therapy at this time. As he later said, he had to indulge this want of hers in order to get what he wanted. He expected it would be brief; he didn't think that coming to therapy would involve a deep commitment.

All three of us met together for three months. Our sessions focused on conflict resolution and improved communication between them. We distinguished between feeling statements ("I feel scared when you walk out the door after a disagreement") and parental control statements ("You shouldn't be talking to so-and-so; it's wrong").

Instead of their conflicts diminishing, they seemed to increase. Their fights became more frequent and, on Jeff's part, more heated. In addition to fighting with Nancy, Jeff became increasingly hostile towards me in our sessions. He misinterpreted my remarks to him and accused me of being insensitive to his needs. He perceived me as "taking Nancy's position." He refused to talk from his feelings, preferring instead to make "head" statements—"You should...That's not realistic...We have different philosophies."

Nancy was familiar with these statements. Characteristically, under stress Jeff became more "intellectual," saying what should be, or telling her what was correct to do—usually what he wanted and she didn't. She had repeatedly run into this invisible but totally effective barricade preventing contact between them.

When she observed the same pattern occurring between Jeff and me, she viewed it more objectively and dispassionately. The longer the three of us talked, the clearer it became that she couldn't force Jeff to be open with her, although she tried.

She had always thought, "If I give in on this point, he'll appreciate me more and want to be closer." The more she had capitulated, the more demanding Jeff had become. Instead of growing closer, they had become polarized.

As she watched Jeff resist a trusting relationship with me, Nancy saw that the difficulties she had tried to avoid in their relationship were out of her control. She stated, "I am unwilling to compromise my integrity by having Jeff tell me who I can be friends with. I've given up a lot already, but I'm afraid I'll lose myself if I don't remember, and hold onto, what's important to me."

By acknowledging that she wasn't responsible for Jeff's peace of mind or for the harmony in their relationship, Nancy let go of the burden she had unconsciously assumed. Without awareness, she had believed that the outcome of this relationship was up to her. When she saw Jeff interact with me the same way he had interacted with her, she saw that he was totally separate from her and that his behavior was his choice. She could "work on the relationship," but in the end she couldn't make him happy. He was responsible for his own happiness.

As Nancy detached from their conflicts, Jeff directed his attention and growing hostility towards me. In his mind, I became responsible for their increased emotional distance, and for his frustration at not being able to influence Nancy.

After several weeks in which Nancy practiced detachment and Jeff grew more angry and more attacking, Nancy decided to separate from him. She moved out of the area and refused to have contact with him. He had become verbally abusive and she was unwilling to participate in that kind of interaction.

Immediately after Nancy's departure, Jeff was furious and punishing towards everyone, but also frantic in his aloneness. He had maintained lots of acquaintances before their marriage, but had gradually lost touch with most of his former pals. When Nancy moved away he terminated our sessions. In his mind I was the cause of this rift and, therefore, an adversary.

Shortly after Nancy's departure, Jeff resumed an old pattern of drug abuse and slacked off at work. His attendance was irregular and his performance, when he was on the job, unpredictable. He was given an ultimatum by his superiors—either enter a drug rehabilitation program or be fired. He had lost his wife and most of his friends. He couldn't tolerate the thought of losing his job, but still he resisted the idea of committing himself to a rehab center. He was not convinced that he had any problems or that he needed to look within himself. He was still satisfied with criticizing others and blaming them for his losses and feelings.

One day after using drugs during his lunch break, he was confronted by his boss, who gave him the choice of either entering a drug rehab program that day or leaving work permanently with no hope of being rehired.

In his depression and hopelessness, Jeff agreed to enter the rehab program. He packed a few clothes, drove there, and was introduced to their program. He later wrote about those first days:

> When I saw the doors of the Center, I freaked. If I go in there I won't ever come out, I thought, and in a way I was right. I didn't know then how much of myself I would have to face.
>
> I looked at those doors for a long time. I was just standing there staring and wondering what I was doing there, when a young man came out and spoke to me. He told me later that my company had called to alert them I was on my way and he was expecting me. They had also told him that I was pretty recalcitrant. He was kind but clear with me. I had smoked a joint in my car on the way down there (My last one, I thought, until I get out of this place so I might as well enjoy it). He must have known but he didn't say anything. He just took my arm and led me into a small room with a bed and a lamp. I lay on the bed the rest of that evening and spoke to no one, even though I heard voices outside my door.
>
> The next day I was scared. I didn't want to be there and I couldn't leave. I didn't want to talk with anyone, but they had compulsory "sharing." A group of druggies sat in a circle and talked about shit from the past and cried. What a bunch of baloney. When they asked me what my story was I told them I didn't have a story, that there was nothing wrong with me, and that I thought they were crazy. I didn't want to have anything to

do with them and I told them so. Everyone jumped on me. I heard the words "denial" and "asshole." I didn't care what they said. I didn't want to hear it or them. I knew why I was there—because I had to be—and I wasn't going to give anyone anything I didn't have to.

I was able to maintain that defense for about five days. I avoided people or snapped at them. If anyone tried to be nice to me I pushed him away. I wasn't going to let those jerks do anything to my mind! But, as time passed, I had a harder time staying cool and in control. I needed my "fix." I found myself in a totally new world—no drugs, no job, no buddies, no way to escape.

After hating everyone and everything I became frantic. How was I going to last a whole month? I knew I couldn't just walk out, but I didn't think I could stay there either.

I was right. I couldn't have stayed there and stayed the way I was. They wouldn't accept the wall I had built around myself. Every morning at sharing time someone would attack me, trying to pick away at the wall. And they were a sharp group. They knew all the games. They had been around the track more times than I had, so I couldn't fool any one of them.

When I didn't want to participate and said I felt sick, they told me to get off it. No excuse worked with them. I couldn't intimidate them, either. I had always been able to scare off anyone else who got too close to me by growling, but these folks just laughed at me and growled back even louder. They were tough! I didn't know what to do. What could I do? I had run all my lines and played all the games I knew, and nobody bought any of them! A few days passed. I thought I had caught on to the game all of them played and I faked it. I would say something about a feeling or my childhood, and then sit back and think I would be ignored for the rest of the session, but I couldn't even get away with that. They called me on everything I said and told me I wasn't being honest. How did they know? I thought I was doing what they wanted. I didn't even know I wasn't being honest. I just kept getting slammed every sharing session we had. They accused me of "stonewalling" and "barricading." I had heard those words before from Nancy but I had never really listened to them. I didn't have to. I just tuned her out. Here, I couldn't escape. These guys had me on the hook and wouldn't let go.

One day, they pushed me so hard that I exploded. I yelled at all of them for several minutes and called them every name I had ever heard. While I was raving at them something happened inside of me and I started crying! I was so damned embarrassed but I couldn't stop. The sobs just kept coming from someplace deep in my gut, and no matter what my head said they just kept coming. I must have bawled there on the floor for twenty minutes. I had never done anything like that before. I had absolutely no control. I couldn't stop the crying or talk or do anything. So I just bawled and moaned and screamed in pain and forgot who I was and where I was. I saw no one and heard nothing else for that time. For those twenty minutes I was somewhere else. I was crazy. I didn't think in words or understand what was happening or use my mind. I was overcome with an unspeakable agony. I had never felt anything like it. It reached to my toes and pulled every part of my insides out with it. I thought I had vomited, but it wasn't physical, just loads of hurt and anger and frustration pouring out of me.

When it all stopped, I was holding my knees and rocking with my head in my arms. I was exhausted. I felt like I had been run over by a train and that it had backed up and run over me again. I couldn't move. I didn't see them, but I became aware that everyone in that group was on the floor with me. When I was calm each one hugged me and spoke to me. I was limp. I couldn't fight them but I didn't hate them. I just wanted to sleep.

When I got to bed I slept for fourteen hours. But instead of feeling stronger when I got up the next day, I felt totally raw. Like someone had scraped away the protective covering on my insides. It hurt to breathe. For the first time I didn't dread the sharing group. Of course, everyone wanted to hear from me first. When I opened my mouth, however, no words would come. Instead I started to cry again! It wasn't the ferocious, violent, gut-wrenching agony from the previous day but a deep wailing. There was some part inside of me where I hadn't ever been before. It gave out with these long, deep . . . well . . . "wails" is the only word I find. It was the strangest experience, almost like I was watching some cord being drawn out of me. It kept coming and coming and I kept wailing. Finally, I only cried. So, I didn't get much talking done that day, either.

Every day that week in group someone said something which got to me. I cried every time! I didn't know I could do that. I felt foolish and a little afraid of what was going to come out of me next, but I was amazed at the same time. Something was happening that I didn't understand. The only experiences I'd had which had been in any way similar to this were when I was taking drugs a lot in school. For a few hours I would be in a different world. All the rules had changed; nothing happened in the same way as when I was straight. In school, when I tripped with my friends, it was fun—going into Oz for a day. We did it enough that I knew what to expect. I'd sit back and watch the show.

But this new show without drugs was more intense than anything I'd done before. I was scared. SCARED! I hated these feelings but that didn't even matter. I wasn't the director. I didn't know what was happening and I couldn't stop it. Every time I walked into that group room the strangest things would happen. I'd walk in as a man and within minutes I'd turn into this sniveling, snot-nosed, whimpering baby. And I couldn't do anything about it. If it hadn't been for the support of the group and the reassurance of Al, our counselor, I would have headed for the hills. This was just too bizarre!

That craziness went on for two weeks. No one reminded me about what a jerk I had been or said anything cruel, like "Who's crazy now?" I deserved it, but they were right there for me when I needed them. Sure, I still felt lousy and wanted to escape, but I couldn't. My surroundings were safe and unchanging. My insides were crazy!

When I thought I couldn't make it or feel one more damned thing, I would talk with Al alone. He had been through all of this himself. He told me about his time on the streets as a junkie for fifteen years, before he cleaned up. He really understood what hell I was in. He wasn't a nice clean therapist in a spiffy office with years of school and diplomas on every wall. The man had stolen and lied and slept in doorways and double-crossed every friend he ever had; and finally he made it. I don't know if I could have made it without him or those guys or the safety of those walls in the rehab center.

Nancy had been an angel to me. I see that now, but I hated myself so much I couldn't stand to have her love me. So I just kept hurting her. I really drove her away. I didn't want anything good or beautiful around me. I knew I didn't deserve it. Now I see it was the guilt I couldn't stand when she loved me. She was so precious and I made her life miserable.

I see now how many people I've hurt throughout my life. Anyone who was decent to me I thought was a sucker. So I took all I could get away with and then left them in the dust. I didn't care. I just thought about how I could get what I wanted.

Boy, being in that drug treatment center sure gave me a different perspective. I had always been so selfish. I didn't even know the word "responsibility." I was living inside my own little shell and when I was uncomfortable I would push someone around or pop a pill. But there's only so long that anyone can get away with that shit. And in that Center it was my time to pay my dues. Boy, did I!

I ended up staying two months. I didn't feel ready to leave when my time was up at the end of one month. I was still pretty shaky and not confident that I could maintain my new-found sobriety. I had learned a lot but I didn't know if it all had sifted down from my head into my blood. I was afraid of a relapse. Not only with the drugs but into my old way of being oblivious to my feelings.

So, I stayed and talked and hung out with Al and watched others go through the cleaning-up process. When I got out, it wasn't a day for wild celebrating, as I had expected it would be. I was scared in a different way from before. Now I just wanted to watch every step, to catch every thought and feeling, and to not kid myself anymore. When I left, they gave me a list of recoverers' meetings—all over the county and on every day and night—that I could attend. I needed that. I didn't trust myself on my own. I knew me too well. I had conned everyone else in my life. I could con myself, too.

Several weeks after Jeff left the treatment center, when he was working again, he called me. We began individual sessions. It had been more than six months since I had talked with him. He didn't seem to have the energy or excitement that was so evident when I had first met him, but his eye contact was steady. He was subdued but not calm. He had done some dramatic work at the rehab center, but he was very well aware that all the pieces weren't in place inside of him. His attendance at work was perfect, but now he was smoking cigarettes continuously and sleeping poorly. He had lost twenty pounds and didn't look well.

This time therapy focused on his early life experiences and the development of the subpersonalities upon whom he later relied, eventually to his own detriment. Jeff told me stories about comforting his alcoholic mother when she cried. Her feelings scared him and he wanted to protect her from them. After she had slept off her binge, she would be hostile and demeaning to him, calling him names and screaming, "Get out of my sight!" His "mushiness," as he termed it, the fear and the wish to help that he had felt when she was incapacitated, was ridiculed when she was sober. He vacillated between identifying with his Boy Scout and his Delinquent. He described himself as "careful, attentive, and helpful" when he was identified with the Boy Scout. When still in that mode of being soft and caring, he would encounter his post-binge mother who was then identified with her Bitch. The Bitch berated and ridiculed the Boy Scout (probably out of guilt, he later thought). But as a kid, Jeff only knew he felt horrible pain from her words. After having been hurt deeply and regularly by her cruel words, he learned not to make himself available for that hurt. He learned to protect himself by not daring to hope that he would be met with appreciation.

He stopped hoping for support, or even for any acknowledgement of his right to be himself. For many years he had hoped that his own unique qualities would be noticed. Being appreciated only when Mom was drunk, and then being deprived of her favor when she no longer needed him, was like having the rug pulled out from under him over and over again. It was done so mercilessly and his pain was so great that, finally, he wouldn't even allow himself to enjoy those moments when Mom did allow closeness (when she was drunk). He closed off that tender part of himself. He no longer wanted or needed kindness. He didn't expect it and wasn't open to receiving it. After so many years of disappointment and betrayal, his Delinquent triumphed in the struggle with the Boy Scout.

Jeff described the Delinquent as an insolent teenaged boy. The chip on his shoulder neared the proportions of a boulder. The Delinquent swaggered, scoffed and mocked. He cared about nothing and no one. He was invulnerable to hurt. He couldn't be affected in any way at all. He had learned that pain always followed closeness and he avoided pain by totally avoiding closeness. No person mattered to him. No achievement was important. Nothing was worth risking humiliation for. This Delinquent learned to protect himself absolutely. Nothing and no one would ever devastate him the way the Boy Scout had been devastated. The Delinquent was self-sufficient and complete unto himself behind his walls.

Jeff could flirt and charm women, but they were only a challenge to him. He seduced them and dropped them. He revelled in his reputation as a "heart-breaker." No woman would ever destroy him. He toyed with women, honing his acting skills expertly, perfecting his role as the Flamboyant Seducer.

By definition, that role had a time limit with any one woman, however. After the seduction, his anxiety increased as his acting skills were exhausted. He had no other part of himself he was willing to share. Therefore, he had to bow out of relationships before any feelings on his part could develop.

Jeff wrote in his journal:

> I didn't know where my heart was during those years. I didn't have any lows. My highs happened when I was acting, and I did get good at that. I was so believable. I could charm the pants off any woman, and that's exactly what I wanted to do. I became known as the Conqueror. I thought it was a joke. Now I see how really angry I had been. I left so many women in tears and I thought I really liked that, but you just don't treat people that way and walk away feeling comfortable about yourself. Still, it did make me feel powerful.
>
> There were so many times in my childhood when I had thought I would collapse because I hurt so much. I hated that in myself. When I saw that weakness in women I thought they were stupid and childish. They asked for it. I didn't ask them to love me.

They just didn't take care of themselves. I had convinced myself that it was every person for himself and that you couldn't blame anyone if you got hurt.

I always solved my "problems" by running away, although I didn't realize it at the time. I saw my feelings as problems and sources of humiliation. I hated myself when I would feel anything. It seemed that when I cared, I got humiliated, and when I wanted someone to like me, I got criticized.

Who needs it? I stopped wanting and stopped hoping I would receive kindness. I became the toughest Bastard around. That saved me from the roller coaster rides that naive Boy Scout always got himself on. I couldn't be destroyed; I couldn't even be touched. I was so far away from where everyone else was, it was funny. They thought that when they talked to me I really cared about what they were saying. I could fool anyone. Disdain became my primary way of relating. No one saw it until a long time after they knew me, though.

Now I see how I was repeatedly punishing Mom for her abandonment of me when I had depended on her. Over and over again, I would get women to depend on me and then I'd toss them away. I knew how that felt and I wanted someone to pay for my agony. Not only could no woman hurt me, I hurt as many of them as I could. Now I see I was doing it all to reinforce my belief in my ability to stand on my own in the world. When my mother would ignore me when I was so young and I needed her, I thought I would die. When I developed my wall, I thought I could live if no pain intruded from the outside world to again hurt me. Then I truly felt powerful if I could make someone else feel pain while I felt nothing. That was what I saw adults doing when I was a kid so I thought I was being just like them. At last I wasn't that hopeless kid anymore. I could play the game.

The drugs helped me maintain that sense of being superman. I tried everything. There wasn't a drug that scared me. My body was invincible. I really thought I had life licked. I was on top of the whole world and no one could push me off. At last I was where I had wanted to be all my life. People looked up to me and I looked down on them.

Even in my marriage I kept myself pretty well defended. I always liked Nancy, but I was careful never to let myself love her or need her. The longer we stayed married, though, the more difficult that became. She was such an innocent. She just kept loving me and taking it upon herself to fix any problems we had. I let her take care of everything. Hell, if that's what she wanted, that was OK with me. She started to change, though. I don't know what it was—the women at work or those self-help books she was always reading—but she slowly started pulling away from me.

I thought it was OK for *me* to act like that, but it was totally *not* OK when I realized that she no longer depended on me. When she started pulling away, I redoubled my efforts to snow her. She's smart, though. She recognized my game and didn't buy my hype. She didn't get hysterical, either, or complain or cry or get hurt. She kept cool and just continued to move away from me.

That drove me crazy. I wasn't the one in control any longer. It was my role to do the leaving. I wasn't the one who was left. But that's just what was happening and I couldn't forestall it any longer! She didn't fall for my gifts or my lines. So all that garbage I had buried finally resurfaced. I attacked her. I said awful things to her and tried to get her to come back to me that way. She used to love a challenge, but now it didn't even tempt her. But then I was inspired! I told her I wanted a child. I knew she wanted one even though she had never said much. This was something she would respond to.

I really did get her attention with that one, too. I thought having a child could help us ignore all the other stuff—what she called communication problems—but she wasn't thrown off the track for more than a day. Instead of smoothing over our problems, they became huge. Now she picked up every little tiny thing I said and did and wanted to know what it meant. "Why was I doing this? What relation to my past did that have?" Cripes! It drove me mad. I totally lost my cool then. She got every bit of leftover resentment and frustration I could find. I dumped it all on her. And when she just backed off I got even crazier!

I drove her away when that was what I most wanted to avoid doing. Every ploy I could think of to hold onto her backfired and I found myself lonelier than I had ever felt in my life.

What a loser I felt like then. But of course no one saw it, or so I thought. I told the guys at work I had asked her to leave. I acted

> like I was glad she was gone. They probably all saw through me. Hell, I was just holding on by my fingertips. I needed drugs then. There was nothing else to depend on.
>
> When my boss faced me at work, I could tell he knew. I had no more excuses, no escapes. Where could I go? What could I say? I had to go to the rehab center, but only because I couldn't turn anywhere else. I had run out of tricks.

I thought our first individual session might be awkward for Jeff but he was unusually clear—in both his eyes and his thoughts. He knew that he had removed a lot of the coverings—the drug abuse, the anger, the violent outbursts—but he also knew he wasn't living comfortably, either. Releasing the symptoms had only made the internal pain clearer. Now, neither the Delinquent nor the Boy Scout prevailed. He had no roles to hide behind. Without the roles he couldn't hide his inner emptiness. Now he was painfully aware of the void inside him. He felt no inner support structure, no frame upon which to hang a personality. He was jelly where he needed a steel column, a solid construction inside him to support his own being, his individuality.

When Jeff described how he felt, I had a sense of possibility now that the clutter had been cleared. He was not opposing the emergence of his own inner truth. Temporarily, he was just experiencing the vacuum between his old defended way of being and the full presence of his authentic self. That's a scary place to be and Jeff was wise to know he needed appropriate support.

We spent part of each therapy session in a guided meditation. By doing that, Jeff had an opportunity to release his identification with his ego roles and to contact a higher self within him. He needed the calm and the perspective this shift afforded him. Through meditating, Jeff learned to look at how he perceived and experienced himself and the world. This awareness became the focus of his meditation sessions.

He noticed what it was like to see through different eyes. Sometimes in our sessions his point of view would shift. He would be aware that he had entered the meditation thinking like a powerless Child, but that he could transcend his identification with that part of himself and see differently.

With his awareness of the gaping inner wound, Jeff acknowledged his unmet need for love, nurturing and consistent support. His Needy Child was very much in evidence when the drugs, the anger and the withdrawal behind the walls were removed. Those had all been ways of hiding that Child.

In his meditations, Jeff encountered that Child's pain. He felt it but at the same time saw it from a higher perspective. In addition to being the Child, he was also the Observer of the Child.

Jeff described his experiences meditating:

> I gradually loosen my hold on my normal way of seeing. I go to another place—usually on my own cloud—and I observe from there. I'm safe and I don't have to protect myself from attack. No one else is a threat to me when I'm there.
>
> Not that it's so pleasant or easy to stay there. No one has ever really been an enemy or the cause of my problems. I could only see that when I got to the cloud. I fought with anyone else to avoid confronting myself. When I face that Needy Child, my heart breaks. I can't seem to comfort him enough to relieve his seemingly never-ending pain.

Only in Jeff's "transcendence" to the cloud could he relate to that Child. He was somewhat removed so that he didn't drown in the Child's emotion. He also could see the Child's boundaries from that perspective; thus, he knew the Child's feelings *did* end at a certain line. The need and the pain weren't limitless. He could choose when and how long he wanted to be with the Child, but he had to spend some time with him every other day. From the cloud he could do it. When he was on the cloud Jeff was calm and anchored, touched by the Child's pain but not overwhelmed by it.

After months of experiencing peace on the cloud, observing the Child, and feeling as much of his pain as he could, Jeff felt stronger.

He wasn't afraid of his inner world and didn't feel compelled to avoid it. The cloud was always present inside and Jeff could consciously go to it when he chose. He did often and began to identify with the peace and the feeling of being centered that it offered. It was now an essential aspect of who he was. He once stated that he was as addicted to the cloud as he had been to drugs or to anger. He had found an inner source of support for his dependency.

More and more frequently, Jeff seemed to speak with a new voice. It was slower and slightly deeper. He paused before he spoke; he was checking inside to hear the words before he verbalized them to another person. Jeff named his new prominent inner subpersonality the Gentle Father. He described what Gentle Father qualities meant to him:

> My mother was so easy to notice and I had thought she was my only significant early relationship. A shame. Because there was *no way* I wanted to be like her. But I did have another parent. How could I ignore him? (Probably because he ignored me.)
>
> Anyway, my corollary inner subpersonality also seemed absent. I think of assertiveness, firmness, clarity and focus as being father qualities. All of those characteristics combine to make strength. Strength comes from inside and it's flexible. My walls used to seem strong to me but they were just rigid. Strength is gentle. As I remove the walls that isolate my Needy Child, the gentle strength slowly emerges. I hear the strength in the new voice that comes out of me sometimes. He's my ideal Father. The first time around (in my real life), I hadn't really experienced having a father, but that wasn't my last chance. Why do we always think that what exists physically is all there ever is?
>
> Now I have a relationship with my inner Gentle Father. He's highly responsible in several ways. He doesn't even want to cheat others; he's not interested in how much he can get away with. He doesn't think of himself as a Loser who has to connive in order to get what he needs. He truly is an adult. When he has commitments to meet, he meets them. They don't scare him. The Delinquent couldn't stand the restrictions he perceived commitments as giving him. Therefore, he always had to be contriv-

ing some undercover deal in his mind. He didn't play fair with anyone; he always had a card he didn't show.

I've always really known that I've acted like a jerk. I was playing a game with the whole world and guess who the chump turned out to be?

The Gentle Father insists that I be honest—with everyone else, too, but basically with myself. He demands that I recognize other people's feelings and respect them.

No more games. That's essentially the message he gives me. No more screwing around. No more living as if what counts comes "later." THIS IS IT. My life is now. He's absolutely committed to being decent—in business and with friends.

Starting with knowing the group in the rehab center and continuing with the people at my meetings, I'm understanding what friendship is. Friends are people you don't have to scam. I can be honest and they still want me around. They don't judge me or compare me or criticize me. They listen to me and want me to listen to them. It's a completely different way of relating from anything I've ever experienced before. I have nothing to gain or lose from them. Nothing material, just the richness of life and being known and being touched.

Now I know what Nancy meant when she said I was untouchable. I was without my Gentle Father. I wasn't centered. I couldn't trust anyone else or myself. I didn't know myself. I wasn't sure I could make it on my own. I was so damned scared! I thought I was protecting myself from being hurt but I was just holding all my old hurts inside. I nurtured them and kept them alive instead of letting them go. I couldn't let in anyone who would love me. I guess I knew that feeling anything new would first involve feeling all those old feelings. I didn't want to do that no matter what the cost!

I only paid that cost at the rehab center when I had enough strong support around me that my world wouldn't fall apart if I did. So I fell apart but, hell, that was the best place I could have done it! Al and the group understood me and didn't let me get away with my shit. Al was the first strong Gentle Father I'd ever known. He really was an honorable man. He looked simple, but he took responsibility for everything he said and did. If I wanted to talk to him he made time for me and really listened. He heard every word I said, but more importantly, he heard me beneath all the words.

He came up against who I really was, and he made me face that person, too. I didn't like what I saw and sometimes he didn't either, but he always accepted me. Yeah, I was a jerk a lot but he knew that I was more than that, too. Being a jerk was just a stupid cover because I was too scared to be honest. Well, he insisted on it. He gave me all he had and he didn't let *me* give any less. He wanted all of me and wouldn't settle for my cover. I couldn't snow him and that saved my life.

Nancy was wonderful but I was killing myself with her. She just wasn't tough enough and that's what I needed. Now my Gentle Father is tough with me. Never vicious, but sometimes brutally honest. I trust his guidance. With Al as a model for awhile and then my sponsor for the meetings, I could find that Gentle Father inside me. Now I talk and listen to him every day. Every day. I don't make a move without consulting him. If I don't follow his guidelines of honesty and responsibility, I pay and the price seems to be getting higher. Deception worked OK when I was a kid but the rules changed sometime when I wasn't looking. Now, it's strictly straight and narrow for me.

Jeff's Gentle Father had always been a subpersonality-in-potential within him, but it took the uncompromising environment of the rehab center for him to actualize it. There, he was forced to confront himself and grow up. He would never have done this without the external demand that he act responsibly. If that had been demanded of him as a young adult, he might have developed his Gentle Father earlier. But all he could do as a kid was to survive in the best way he could. So he did that with the Delinquent. That was the very best protection he could muster. He needed that defense and it had worked for him. He did as well as he could at the time.

He paid for his safety, though, with his immaturity and his inability to relate intimately. When one way-of-being stops working for us—and it always does at some point if it's based on a very young understanding of the world—we can find an older, wiser subpersonality inside. We need to switch our allegiance and identification, and allow an adult responsibility to prevail in our lives. Our childhood basis for living cannot possibly encompass our adult talents and needs. As children we usually have very little inner strength going for us and a lot of dependency on the external adults. If the adults around us have their own hang-ups (and who doesn't?), we adjust. We don't know we're doing this; we just learn to live however we must. Whatever subpersonality helps us to do that successfully is favored.

When we cling to one subpersonality, we ignore others and prevent inner integration and growth. We live incompletely. However, we usually find that life itself puts an end to that incomplete way of living. As long as we need to cut off parts of ourselves in order to survive, we seem to be allowed that leeway. But sometimes—often in our late twenties to fifties—our manipulations cease to provide the rewards they once did. Parents are no longer around and the world has a way of pointing out our distortions. Our manipulations cease to be effective. Everything we "know" becomes useless. We now must release the defenses which have kept us unaware of some part/s of us, and look at what we've feared.

Life has a way of deciding for us when our time of reckoning is. Our arguments or protestations are irrelevant. When it's time to face ourselves, it's time. It seldom happens all at once and it never happens without the support we need—outside or inside—being available. No one has ever died from letting repressed pain come out. And after we've felt it, we can integrate the parts of ourselves we've cut off. We thought we couldn't survive with them during the first part of life; now we can't survive wholly without them. The authenticity which follows from our openness to ourselves allows us to live fully and richly. Without our fears or hurts limiting us, we can allow life to guide us and to provide us with the experiences we need. Being fully and flexibly human is the goal, and life will give us the experiences we need to get there—if we don't resist!

Which subpersonality did you rely on most when you were young?

_____
_____
_____

Which subpersonalities did you hide when you were young?

_____
_____
_____

How do you hide your Needy Child?

_____
_____
_____
_____
_____
_____

Which subpersonality do you currently identify with, and which do you project on to others?

_____
_____
_____
_____
_____
_____
_____
_____

Think of one relationship you have and describe your interactions in terms of each person's subpersonalities. Each of you may identify with several subpersonalities at different times in your interactions. What have you noticed?

_____
_____
_____
_____
_____
_____
_____
_____
_____

Who is a mature subpersonality with whom you need to stay in touch?

_____
_____
_____

What kinds of things does that subpersonality tell you?

_____
_____
_____
_____
_____
_____
_____
_____

Relaxation

Do the relaxation exercise on page 9.

Exercise

Let an image come to you. This image symbolizes an ongoing struggle which two of your subpersonalities maintain. (*Pause.*) Watch. (*Pause.*) Who are the two subpersonalities? (*Pause.*) Notice the characteristics of their interaction. (*Pause.*)

Allow the interaction to continue and notice that your soul ascends out of that scene to a cloud directly above these two interacting subpersonalities. (*Pause.*) How does it feel to be on that cloud? (*Pause.*) From that cloud, look at whatever you see around you. What do you notice? (*Pause.*) Just breathe and experience being on that cloud. (*Pause.*)

Remaining on the cloud, look down at the two subpersonality figures. (*Pause.*) Notice each figure from the cloud perspective. (*Pause.*) What do you notice about their interaction from this perspective that you couldn't see from below? (*Pause.*)

Descend directly from the cloud into the scene with the two figures. (*Pause.*) You have brought with you your experiences from the cloud. Notice what happens in the scene. (*Pause.*) Is there a shift or a change? (*Pause.*) If some kind of resolution occurs, notice how it happens. (*Pause.*)

Who were your two interacting subpersonality figures?

_____
_____
_____

What was their interaction about?

_____
_____
_____
_____
_____
_____
_____
_____
_____

How did it feel being on the cloud?

_____
_____
_____

What did you see when you looked around you?

_____
_____
_____

How did the two figures look from that perspective?

_____
_____
_____
_____
_____

Did you notice anything from the cloud that you hadn't seen before?

After the soul descended from the cloud, was there a shift or a resolution? Describe what happened.

Listening to Spirit   8

Sally is a Catholic Sister. She entered the convent after high school when she was seventeen. At thirty-four, she had chronic mononucleosis, long lasting colds and migraines. As a child, Sally had been a mother to her mother. When Sally was ten, her mother became ill for two years after a difficult birth. Sally cared for the new baby and for her mother. Whenever Sally wasn't available to her mother, she would be called "selfish." In order to avoid that damning label, Sally made herself available to her mother for everything at any time.

In the convent after college, Sally taught grade school and then went into social work. She did counseling in a residential treatment center. Again, Sally was available to everyone anytime. She was constantly exhausted but didn't consider taking time off. "No" was not in her vocabulary.

In her convent living situation, Sally was thrust into contact with many Sisters. Being introverted by nature, Sally experienced this constant interaction with others as draining. She often felt frustrated and impatient with Sisters who were inconsiderate, but she felt that this was a personal fault which she tried to overcome. Life for Sally was a challenge in every area. There was no place she could relax and let go. She always felt pressured to "be nice." She told herself that she should be able to take care of others all the time.

In our meetings, Sally was slow to trust. At our first session, she stated flatly, "I don't want to talk about my mother or my vocation." I honored her request but noted her two forbidden subjects. She told me about her work days and her nights at the convent. If I were to offer any words of support recognizing her strain, she would brush them away defensively, assuring me that I didn't understand, that nothing was wrong.

Building a trusting relationship took almost three years. It was slow and painful work. Sally would not consider terminating therapy because she was convinced there was something wrong with her that she needed to fix. Her experiences in close relationships had always led her to feel criticized and judged. The best way she had found to avoid these painful alternatives was to give to others and put their needs first. In this way, she could keep them comfortable and perhaps avoid their ire. She constantly looked around her, assessing the comfort of people in her environment. She looked like a frightened bird with her darting eyes and her shallow breath.

Sally projected onto me her expectations of being abused. She would usually stand in the hall until I invited her to come into the office. She entered with her head and eyes lowered. Often she wouldn't start speaking unless I asked her a question. When I didn't start the sessions for her, she would sit uncomfortably for several minutes as though she wanted to speak but felt compelled not to speak first. She had rules for herself of which I was unaware.

One of her rules, I later learned, was that in any situation she had to comply. In our sessions, therefore, she thought that she had to let me set the tone. In the convent, she had to allow the other Sisters to do what they wanted, however it affected her. At work, she had to take care of the needs of the residents. She was alive simply to make others comfortable.

Sally looked ten years older than she was, due to the dark circles around her eyes and her emaciated form. At times, when she would miss a session due to illness or during a session when she would complain of fatigue, I would try to explore with her what she could do to take care of her health. She seemed to view me as a heathen, trying to pull her away from serving God. Her suffering led her to feel holy and, in a roundabout way, smug. She was profiting too much from suffering to consider alternative ways to live.

It was only after I learned more about Sally's inner world figures that I fully understood her fear. We talked about her life and then her feelings for months, not considering any divergent approaches which would upset her preconception of therapy.

As Sally realized the difference between thinking and feeling, she acknowledged that her feelings didn't operate according to her intellect's rules. We spoke in feeling words and learned what was psychologically meaningful to her. We discussed how her mind had made sense of her experience, how she had learned what to do in relationships. Sally developed a context for understanding her feeling world.

After we had laid this basis for approaching her inner world, we talked in terms of subpersonalities. After the months of introduction to her inner world, Sally could accept this concept of different parts of herself who had different goals and different needs.

With the diligence Sally employed to attack any task, she approached her inner world figures. Because she finally trusted me, she was willing to consider trusting her inner process, the dynamics among her subpersonalities. She listened, somewhat fearfully at first, hearing nothing for many weeks. But she would never give up on a task once she had accepted it, so regardless of the lack of results, she persisted. She focused very precisely on her inner world. She would start by breathing and letting her mind calm down from her chronic busyness. Then she would find a feeling and let it develop and grow and fill her. She wouldn't fight it or try to analyze it; she would just allow it to be. By welcoming it and even encouraging it to grow larger, Sally acknowledged the reality of whichever subpersonality was prominent at the time. With acceptance, the subpersonality no longer had to maneuver in a hidden, sneaking manner avoiding her conscious awareness. Since Sally was willing to know her subpersonalities (as she had finally been willing to be known by me), they revealed themselves to her. (Subpersonalities are very sensitive little beings; if they think that you don't want to know them, they won't intrude on your conscious awareness.)

The first subpersonality who spoke to her was the Suffering Servant. After many minutes of listening attentively, some words became faintly audible:

Servant: You really should be helping others. It doesn't seem right for you to be sitting here, doing nothing. People need your efforts, your work.

Adult: I'm taking time to listen.

Servant: Listen to what? You know you should be giving others what they need. That's why you are on this earth.

Adult: So I have to produce work to justify my existence. Is that what you're saying?

Servant: We all do. Work now and your reward will come later.

Adult: I should work for a future reward? 'Then' will be different from 'now'?

Servant: If you work now and serve others you can make it be different. You have to earn salvation.

Adult: I have to do something in order to be saved?

Servant: Yes, work and help others and you will be rewarded.

Sally thanked the Suffering Servant and breathed and sat quietly. She allowed the Suffering Servant to speak to her and for three months this was the only voice she heard. Then, after one of the Suffering Servant's usual responses with Sally again thanking it and sitting quietly, she heard another voice. After hearing the words clearly, she could identify this voice as the Punitive Parent. It spoke to her:

Parent: You ought to be ashamed of yourself. Everyone else is working and you're loafing.

Adult: You want me to be different?

Parent: I want you to quit being selfish. You only think about what you want and how you feel. You're disgusting!

Adult: I'm feeling guilty.

Parent: You should be. If you were doing something productive, you'd feel better.

Sally listened to the Punitive Parent tell her to be productive for another two months before she responded:

Adult: Being productive never has taken away unpleasant feelings for very long before.

By confronting her inner Punitive Parent, Sally realized that she didn't have to give power to this subpersonality who was criticizing her. She could stand up for herself. That she could do this was a revelation for Sally. When she stood up to that inner, critical, Punitive Parent and didn't swallow everything which that subpersonality said to her, she felt stronger and more able to take care of herself.

Without any conscious decision, she noticed her responses to her Superiors changing, too. When, unconsciously, she sensed that she was in a position similar to the one with the inner Punitive Parent, i.e., being criticized and being treated as though she were powerless, she found herself responding in a self-affirming way. When a Superior would ask her to do more than she felt she could, she would decline. If she were called selfish or insensitive, she would respond that she was neither, but that she simply couldn't do anymore. She didn't allow anyone outside or inside of her to demean her.

When she first noticed herself acting in this self-affirming way, she was surprised. She had no need to be in conflict with the other Sisters, but she did have a strong need to protect herself. She had learned to do that by listening to, and engaging in dialogue with, her inner Punitive Parent. When she took care of herself in that inner relationship, she did so in her outer relationships without any conscious effort or fear. This change delighted her. It was a realization more than a decision. When she stopped playing the role of Helpless Child to her inner authoritative Punitive Parent, she didn't assume that role with anyone in her external world, either.

Sally was encouraged and excited by these outer reflections of her inner work. She had affected her daily life experience by adjusting her consciousness; she no longer encountered external Punitive Parents. She began to grasp the connection between her inner identifications and her outer interpersonal experience. This increased her sense of power significantly.

During her quiet periods of listening, another voice became clear, the Driver. After a few conversations with the Driver, his pattern became clear to Sally. He usually gave her a list of things to do:

Driver: If you start now you can finish the sewing and the book keeping before supper and maybe get some letters written.

Adult: You always have things for me to do.

Driver: Just do the sewing, the bookkeeping, and the letters, and then you can rest.

Adult: I don't trust you. You've told me that before, "Only do these three things," and then I do them and I never get to rest more than a few minutes.

Driver: Well, work fast and get everything done and then you can take all the time you want.

After a few weeks, Sally was well enough acquainted with the Driver to know that his list was endless. Any end to the chores was temporary. He seemed to be able to compile jobs that were urgent without end. Always there was the promise, "Just these three more things and then it will be all over," but Sally had heard that so much with never a real break that she no longer trusted his promises.

So, again, she followed her breath and waited. Sally did this exercise of breathing and listening daily. Often the dialogues were similar. Once in a while, she might hear from her Child or her Aching Body. But usually it was her Suffering Servant, Punitive Parent or Driver subpersonality who spoke to her. By listening to them, Sally acknowledged their existence and their wants.

Sally didn't deny them or push them away, but she stopped identifying with them. She didn't jump up and do what the Suffering Servant, the Punitive Parent or the Driver suggested. She listened to them and acknowledged them and followed her breathing. By doing this Sally learned that she was not equivalent to whoever her loudest subpersonality was at any given time. Just because she heard a voice forcefully did not mean that it was wise or that it was working in her long-term best interest. She just noticed the voices and returned to her breathing.

She noticed that the voices softened and changed as she treated them respectfully but with caution. She didn't give any voice ultimate power. She didn't need approval from any particular subpersonality. When she owned her power by not letting her subpersonalities send her scurrying, she could maintain a sense of being "above the fray," as she termed it. She observed but didn't act.

By continuing this practice, Sally became aware of deeper intuitions. Her subtle voices had to be assured that Sally wanted to hear from them. She had to create an inner quietness and receptivity before they would speak to her. As she could do this frequently, she began to notice "quiet wisdom."

During Sally's quiet moments, a re-evaluation of the meanings of responsibility and morality seemed to be occurring without her thinking mind being involved. She wrote in her journal:

> I've wanted so deeply to make the world better, to contribute to the good of the whole, to reduce suffering. I thought that I should do these things. That was what being a good Christian was about. I wanted to do my part. I've always felt frustrated, though, because I could never do enough. I would wear myself out working as hard as I could and still there would be poverty and suffering, not only in the world but in my neighborhood where I'm working.
>
> I'm not looking for fast results or even necessarily for tangible rewards, but have I really been doing anything other than just responding to those voices inside which tell me to stay busy? Am I making myself sick for the sake of some neurotic subpersonality? I'm willing and eager to suffer if that will make the world better or if God wants it for some unseen purpose, but have I created a world, made up of some wacky characters who tell me rigid rules and then punish me so that I can have some convoluted way to be right? Have I wanted to be right so much that I've organized a

way to be right on my own? Have I just made this whole thing up?

Am I keeping myself sick by following some rules that someone in my head thought up? What if God doesn't care if I accomplish a lot of work? What if it's the Driver I'm trying to please and not God at all?

Is the Driver God's representative in my head? Or is the Driver a leftover from my mother who would punish me if I weren't busy? Am I making myself sick to keep my mother happy, when I don't even see her anymore? Sometimes I feel so driven and I act so compulsively! I'm acting out of some old played-over-and-over tape, which tells me to stay frantically busy.

Am I creating God in Mom's image? Does God want the same thing from me that she did? She was always easier on me when I was sick, so being sick had some rewards. Does God want me to be sick? Is being good in my relationship with God the same as being good in the relationship with my mother? What does having a relationship with God mean? In my other relationships, I don't figure out what relating to my friend means and then compulsively act that way forever and ever. I sit and talk and listen. Really, having relationships that are truly friendships has only happened in this last year. Before, I was too busy doing something in order to avoid feeling guilty. I didn't value spending time with other people enough to have friendships develop. OK, so I have several friendships now with people. What does having a relationship with God mean?

Well, first I have to be open to know God. To get to know my friends, I set aside time and I listen to them. When I was getting to know all the voices inside of me, I listened to them. Listening to God seems to be the first step in having a relationship. Who is He? Or is He She? When I think of God as She, I think of my mother and the Superiors in the convent. They have been Drivers. Can I separate God from them? I've been treating God as just another autocratic authority. I hate it when people generalize about me, thinking that they know me because they know I'm a Sister. Knowing one thing about me doesn't make them know me. And knowing some other authority doesn't mean I know God.

> OK, so how do I get to know God? Well, listen. So, what do I listen to? The priest's Sunday sermons? Yuck! It's getting increasingly difficult for me to listen to other humans tell me what is right and how I'm bad and what I should do. I don't want to hear that from God.
>
> In my own mind, I've made God in my mother's image. What if I've created God? Well, the good part about that is I can un-create Him. So, I want to listen without preconceived notions in order to get to know Him. What an interesting idea! Just listen.
>
> When I stop and breathe and listen, I hear from all those other voices. Now, I know that none of them is God. They are just their own personalities. Just as God isn't the same as any person I've known, He is not the same as any of my subpersonalities. They have been formed as my reaction to other people or situations, or as my way of getting through some tight spots. Nothing eternal or wise about that. Just a way of getting by. God must be deeper and wiser than any of my other voices. I'll just sit and listen and when I hear other voices I can identify, I'll let them go. Then maybe I'll get deeper, closer to who God really is.

And so, Sally resumed her sitting and breathing and listening. Usually she would hear from one or more subpersonalities as she settled into a state of inner stillness. She was able to let those voices go and to return her attention to her breath.

After several months of doing this Sally wrote:

> My times alone, being still, are becoming more and more important to me. They seem to be vital now. It's at those times I feel most alive, most connected with the world, most receptive to God's will. And my experience of God's will isn't like anything I've experienced with any human person. I don't hear a voice that says, "Do this and don't do that."
>
> It's mostly just a "knowing" I have. Sometimes my hands become tingly and I trust that God is telling me He is with me. Sometimes they don't and I don't have any manifestation of His presence except that I know everything's OK. "God's in His heaven, all's right with the world." I know all's not right with the world, but in another way, it is. I don't have to clean up messes and I

> don't have to make other people's lives turn out right and I don't even have to make anyone happy.
>
> In a way it sounds very selfish. (Isn't that funny? For me, finding God lay in embracing that quality which I was taught most to hate—selfishness.) It's selfish because I don't take it upon myself to change the world or even to show another person what truth really is. I just value so much those moments when I can be quiet and listen and be with God.
>
> I enjoy my times with others more. There seems to be a love which is larger than all of us which blankets us. We can move together or apart and still be covered by that love. And being covered by that love makes everything else less urgent. His love is with us all. So what are we working for? Not to earn acceptance; we already have it.
>
> He's not asking me to fly around, knocking myself out. Now I can differentiate very well between the knowing I feel in His presence and my mind's injunctions to "do something."
>
> Sometimes I feel the need to do something, but not out of a desperation, a struggle or a hope that this act will make me OK or safe. If I feel pulled to act, it's to do the act, not to earn a reward or make something else happen, but just to do whatever I feel called to do. And then I can let it go because I have no investment in how it turns out. I was just called to do it and so I do it and then walk away and wait to be called again.
>
> My life is much calmer; the peace is deeper than anything I've known. And it is all from my listening inside. Beneath the voices, there is truth. The wisdom is in not being caught up in the voices, in *not doing*. For me wisdom lies in my willingness to just be.

By listening to and knowing her own subpersonalities, Sally was able to move beyond them into a realm that wasn't just personal. In this deeper, transpersonal realm, her experience was not related to her past. It was an arena broader than her individual feelings. She realized the universality of human experience and felt her identification with the larger whole. She stopped viewing others in terms of their identifications with their dominant subpersonalities. Since she could see beyond her own subpersonalities, she could also appreciate that there was a greater depth to others.

She experienced God by living at this level of union and connectedness. Her own identification with any one subpersonality previously had prevented her from living at this level.

Sally had always been concerned with moral action, but after her therapy experience, she described morality as balancing the needs she heard from all of her subpersonalities, being willing to feel all of her feelings (not only the "acceptable" feelings), and allowing her inner world to guide her. Spirituality was no longer separated from her body experience. It was not concerned with an ideal concept of how she thought she should be. Spirituality for Sally became living her bodily life responsibly and with commitment to her inner world. She placed authority for making decisions within herself and developed a new conscience. No longer was her conscience a set of rules someone older had taught her long ago. Now Sally experienced her conscience as her body experience which let her know when something she was doing or considering wasn't good for her. She valued her body as her seat of wisdom. No longer could she oppress its voice and use illness as a way to avoid knowing herself.

Sally grew into freedom. It wasn't license to do everything, but a strong sense of her purpose in life on a daily basis. Her health improved steadily. Now, if she is not feeling healthy and vibrant, she knows that she needs to ask inside which subpersonality needs her attention.

Have you thought about responsibility as starting inside you?

_____
_____
_____

For you, what would being responsible to your inner world mean that you would do?

How do you maintain a relationship with God, a higher power or your higher self?

Relaxation

Spend several minutes doing the relaxation exercise on page 9.

Exercise

Let an image come to you symbolizing your body. *(Pause.)* Let an image come to you symbolizing your mind. *(Pause.)* Let an image come to you symbolizing your feelings. *(Pause.)*

You stand at the base of a mountain with the three parts that you have just imagined—your body, mind and feelings. You are going to take them up the mountain. Have them join hands, or connect in some other way. *(Pause.)* Notice how they interact. *(Pause.)* Walk up the mountain and notice how the journey proceeds. *(Pause.)* What do you notice about each part of you? *(Pause.)* Watch them move up the mountain. *(Pause.)*

As you near the top of the mountain a habitat becomes apparent. Notice the details of this dwelling. *(Pause.)* A Wise Person lives here and comes out now to speak to you and your body, mind and feelings. *(Pause.)* What do you notice about the Wise Person? *(Pause.)* What is the gender, the appearance, the clothing of the Wise Person? *(Pause.)* How does the Wise Person move? *(Pause.)*

The Wise Person approaches your group, turns to your body, and gives it a message which offers guidance. Listen. *(Pause.)* Then the Wise Person turns to your mind and delivers some words of guidance to that part. Listen. *(Pause.)* Then the Wise Person turns to your feelings and offers words of guidance to that part. Listen. *(Pause.)* Finally the Wise Person turns to you and speaks to you. Listen. *(Pause.)* If anyone wants to ask the Wise Person a question allow that to happen now. *(Long pause.)* Have each of the four of you thank the Wise Person, turn, and begin the journey down the mountain. *(Pause.)* Watch how this journey proceeds. *(Pause.)* Notice how the parts interact with each other. *(Pause.)* Notice if the walk down is easy or difficult compared to the walk up the mountain. *(Pause.)* Returning to the base of the mountain, have all four of you touch or connect somehow. *(Pause.)* Watch. *(Pause.)* Notice the relationships among the four of you now. *(Pause.)* Say goodbye and follow your breathing.

What were the representations for you, your body, mind and feelings?

_____
_____
_____
_____
_____
_____
_____
_____
_____
_____
_____
_____

How did they interact?

_____
_____
_____
_____
_____
_____

How did you relate to them?

_____
_____
_____
_____
_____

Describe the habitat at the top of the mountain:

_____
_____
_____
_____
_____
_____

Describe the Wise Person:

_____
_____
_____
_____
_____
_____

What messages did the Wise Person give to the body, mind, feelings and you?

_____
_____
_____
_____
_____

Describe the trip down the mountain:

At the end, when you reached the base of the mountain, what did you notice about the relationships among the body, mind, feelings and you?

_____

_____
_____

At the end, when you reached the base of the mountain, what did you notice about the relationships among the body, mind, feelings, and you?

_____
_____
_____
_____
_____
_____
_____
_____

Afterword

Life isn't meant to be continually frustrating or painful. Sometimes it is, of course, and at those times we can't avoid it. We do well to feel the frustration and pain and just breathe through it.

The body and one's life experiences provide sources of wisdom. They offer us the guidance we need. It is not written out for us or delivered in quickly understandable words. Our unconscious wants to communicate with us, but we must learn to speak its language.

A marvelous drama is always available to us—our subpersonalities are constantly living and experiencing, feeling and deciding. And they want to be known by us.

Getting to know our inner selves takes a great deal of time and commitment. We can't determine what we will hear when we listen. That is where the "letting go" phase of knowing ourselves comes in. Let go of previously held restrictions and say, "Whatever is there I welcome." Then allow yourself to be guided and trust your inner wisdom.

Messages from the unconscious are gifts which are offered to help us. These unconscious messages come to us through our subpersonalities, and through dreams and images. From the exercises in the text, you have received some awareness of your inner selves. You have noticed the concerns of different parts of you and the methods they have used to take care of themselves. You have also heard the guidance from the Wise Person and the ceiling figure. Now that you've done these exercises, congratulate yourself. You have truly made a major commitment to knowing yourself.

Now, continue to spend time with each figure within you. Just listen. Don't talk except to ask questions. Allow the figure to talk to you. Form relationships with the subpersonalities as though they were new friends. Get to know them. Don't judge them or try to change them. Listen and accept them.

You will notice that as your inner relationships strengthen, your subpersonalities change. Just watch. They are your children. Love them and give them what they need to grow. Even if they are horrid to you, stay with them and listen. Hear their feelings behind their words. Listen to the subpersonalities interact with each other. Notice their relationships, who predominates, who withdraws, what imbalances are apparent. Just be aware. If you do this once a day, at a regular time, you will inevitably see changes in your life. Your inner selves will come to trust you and share great insights with you. They will have a forum in which to interact and grow. You may also want to repeat the exercises after you have been listening to your subpersonalities for several months. You will probably meet new inner figures with different, perhaps more subtle, concerns.

This process of attending to your inner world needs to be integrated into your life. These figures are as important as anyone you will contact during the day. Your caring about them is transformative. Healing will occur when you are silent, focus inside and allow your inner life to lead you.

Your subpersonalities will offer you many gifts: joy, peace and true vitality—a deep, wise aliveness that comes from your center and leads you beyond yourself.

Glossary

AUTHORITY	The person/s or figures upon whom we depend for physical or emotional safety and comfort.
CONSCIOUS	What we are aware of thinking or doing.
DENIAL	A defense mechanism by which the mind refuses to acknowledge what is, interiorly or exteriorly.
DETACHMENT	Watching another's, or our own, experience from a viewpoint separated from feelings, thoughts or a need to control the outcome.
EGO	In both the conscious and the unconscious, the ego is that part of us that wills, controls and sees ourselves as being separate from others. It is neither good nor bad, only a necessary part of each human.

GOOD	In this text, "good" describes the characteristics we adopt to please childhood authorities—parents, guardians, teachers or our notion of God. It implies an inauthentic way of being in that we promote one subpersonality and hide others rather than being totally self-disclosing and allowing whatever consequences occur.
IDENTIFY	Aligning our feelings and thoughts with one way of being and failing to acknowledge alternatives.
IMAGERY	Images may be seen or thought or "known" (intuited). They are pictures our unconscious gives us in order to communicate with us.
INNER WORLD	There is a reality inside of each of us which is not physical and which constitutes the essence of who we are as unique individuals.
PASSIVE-AGGRESSIVE	Indirectly hostile behavior you don't take responsibility for.
POWER	The sense of personal effectiveness we have when we are living in accordance with our inner needs.
PROJECTION	A subpersonality we don't want to see inside of ourselves, so we see it in others. Usually we have a strong reaction, positive or negative, to another person when we project onto him or her. When we own a projection, we don't focus our attention on another person. We look inside of ourselves to see how what we are being shown is true about ourselves.

REPRESSION	Unconsciously, material is pushed out of awareness and buried in the personal unconscious usually because it is too threatening to our psychological equilibrium.
SAFETY	Young beings need the assurance of physical survival. Because the young are totally dependent, unconsciously their first concern is survival/safety.
SHADOW	The parts of ourselves we choose not to see, and which we repress into the unconscious.
SUB-PERSONALITIES	The different energies or patterns of acting and feeling within us. We all have very many subpersonalities. Given a nurturing environment they grow and mature. New ones appear at certain times or in certain situations.
SURRENDER	Releasing our resistance to the experiences, inner and outer, that life brings us.
TRANSCEND	To loosen our ego identifications so that we may rise above our mental and emotional ways of perceiving.
TRANSPERSONAL	The realm which is greater than the individual and includes soul or spirit.
UNCONSCIOUS	The part of us of which we are neither aware nor in control. The personal unconscious contains all the material we have repressed. The collective unconscious refers to partici

pation in the greater whole, not associated with personal histories. It envelopes and unites everything alive.

VITALITY — Being open to all parts of ourselves and willing to hear whatever they give us. It does not imply excitement, only honesty, receptivity and surrender.

ORDER FORM

☐ *PLEASE SEND ME A FREE CATALOG*

Name_____

Address_____

City_____ State_____ Zip_____

Quantity	Book Title and Author	Price	Total
	Good People: The Whole Self Integration Guide by Ruth Cherry, Ph.D.	$12.95	
	Master Meditations: A Spiritual Daybook by Dr. Donald Curtis	12.95	
	The Book of Rituals: Keys to Personal and Planetary Transformation by Rev. Carol Parrish-Harra	19.95	
	The New Age Handbook on Death & Dying by Rev. Carol Parrish-Harra	9.95	
	When Your Parents Need You: A Caregiver's Guide by Rita Robinson	9.95	
	Survivors of Suicide by Rita Robinson	9.95	
	Being Human in the Face of Death edited by Deborah Roth, MSC & Emily LeVier, MSC	9.95	
	Stepping Stones to Grief Recovery edited by Deborah Roth, MSC	8.95	
	The Law of Mind in Action by Dr. Fenwicke Lindsay Holmes	10.95	
	The Laws of Wealth by Dr. Fenwicke Lindsay Holmes	10.95	
	AIDS: A Self-Care Manual (Third Edition) by AIDS Project Los Angeles	14.95	
	When Someone You Love Has AIDS by BettyClare Moffatt, MA	8.95	
	Gifts for the Living: Conversations with Caregivers on Death & Dying by BettyClare Moffatt, MA	9.95	

SUBTOTAL _____

SALES TAX 6.5%
(California Only) _____

SHIPPING/HANDLING
($2.00 per book) _____

TOTAL DUE _____

Please send check or money order to:

**IBS PRESS, INC.
744 Pier Avenue
Santa Monica, CA 90405
(213) 450-6485**

— — — — — — — — — — FOLD ALONG DOTTED LINE — — — — — — — — — — — —

| PLACE |
| STAMP |
| HERE |

IBS PRESS, INC.
744 PIER AVENUE
SANTA MONICA, CA 90405